Ron Sunner

COMMITTED COMMUNITIES

COMMITTED COMMUNITIES

FRESH STREAMS
FOR WORLD MISSIONS

CHARLES J. MELLIS

William Carey Library

1705 N. SIERRA BONITA AVE. • PASADENA, CALIFORNIA 91104

Library of Congress Cataloging in Publication Data

Mellis, Charles J
  Committed Communities.
  Bibliography: p.
  1. Christian communities. 2. Missions. I. Title.
BV4405.M44   267   76-53548
ISBN 0-87808-426-6

Third Printing, 1983

Copyright © 1976 by Charles J. Mellis

Published by
William Carey Library
P. O. Box 40129
1705 N. Sierra Bonita Ave.
Pasadena, California 91104
Telephone (213) 798-0819

PRINTED IN THE UNITED STATES OF AMERICA

To

John and Jim

who, by their timely emergence into adulthood,
lovingly launched me on the tortuous journey

. . . of learning to listen.

Contents

viii

Foreword

You can almost hear the ticking as you read. The bomb may go off before you finish. This is an idea whose time has come. It is an idea that bursts out of the mediocre present to pose a significant breakthrough in new means and power of outreach, just as the splitting of the atom ushered in a new era in conventional warfare.

Something else. Rarely, very rarely, do you find a truly weighty, even mind-boggling concept presented in such sprightly, delightful directness. The author is as uncommon as the book: impressed but not overawed by routine, well-worn patterns of interpretation, he exploits the practical insights of much experience in a leadership position in a globe-girdling organization, distills a great deal out of his serious study and research, and adds to all this a huge amount of truly keen, personal perception.

He shows the way forward. And in eminently practical terms. But he builds his case by a fascinating *tour de force* of the data of our entire experience since the days of the apostles. This is no rootless scheme! In brief: a rich, rewarding, truly exciting and relevant book. Wait till this gets out, sinks in. We'll all see the results. You can hear the ticking as you read.

Ralph D. Winter

Pasadena, California
October, 1976

Preface

This book is addressed *to* my peers. But I also wrote it *for* committed young adults who seek an authentic way to share their faith with the world.

I see my peers as the decision makers of cross-cultural (nee "foreign" or "overseas") missions. This decision-making certainly is not limited to official boards, executives and administrative staffs. The pastor of every mission-hearted congregation, and the lay people who rotate on and off its missionary committee, exert more influence than they realize — particularly when change is called for. And it is a thesis of this book that *some* structural changes are needed — in fact are probably overdue. So I'm addressing this to all of you, as one of you.

My younger brothers and sisters: I trust you'll excuse me when I turn to talk directly to my peers. (For one thing, it saves a lot of clumsy literary devices.) But please don't leave the room or wander off. I *want* you to eavesdrop. And if you identify with what you find in these pages, I hope you'll bug us to make it happen. I'm sure you'll give us a reasonable period of time to work out the changes. But if it becomes clear that we're digging in our heels, seek the Spirit's guidance and make it happen yourselves. (Chapter 9 may give you some practical help in getting started.)

My aim is not to preach commitment, but to propose viable new channels for it. I assume that you who read this book are committed — an assumption I cannot make for all Christians. In fact, another thesis of this book centers around a realistic recognition that

Christians vary widely in their levels of commitment; and the expansion of Christianity has always depended on the obedience of the deeply-committed few.

A corollary to this thesis sees the vital, structured communities of this committed minority as essential flesh-and-blood organs of the Body of Christ, not artificial prosthetic devices. And it is in such communities, marked by commitment to one another, and by a shared commitment to a task, that this minority has most often made its impress on history. The committed community with a life of its own has repeatedly served the Church as a whole, both as a renewing vanguard and as the arms and legs of its outreach.

In addition to establishing these theses (the latter via biblical and historical models), I have sought to describe the environment in which they must be applied today. This involves not only a candid look at our current missionary agencies as they have evolved from nineteenth century models, but also a view of American society based on the development of certain sub-cultural streams. Here I have not sought a complete analysis; nor have I sought to "prove" the superiority of any one application. I do have some opinions, and I have shared them. These may turn out to be no more than seed thoughts. Some of you may push on from there and develop even more viable options. Great!

But new options we must have — whether as supplements to, or modifications of, our present structures — if we are to absorb the human energy potential that we have and need for sharing our faith with the world.

Introduction

I was in my mid-30's before I became a baseball fan. Three things converged in 1958 to make it happen. Our family returned from our second overseas assignment. Our two oldest boys, at 12 and 10, were "ripe" for bubble-gum baseball cards — and more. And that's the year the Dodgers moved to Los Angeles. With the Giants also moving to San Francisco, major league fever hit the West Coast and quickly became an epidemic.

With the Dodgers came Vince Scully. Now to Dodger fans, Vinny is the unquestioned dean of sportscasters. (Come-lately's like Cosell leave us cold.) Vin tried to verbalize for his new western fans how it was that the stumbling, fumbling Bums from Brooklyn could become world champions — particularly against that efficiency factory of baseballdom: Casey Stengel's Yankees. The Yankees, after all, had a whole bench full of sluggers who could hit the long ball — and hit it out. A "Dodger home run," by contrast, consisted of bunting for a base hit, stealing second, taking third on a passed ball, and scoring on a sacrifice fly!

The difference, Vinny told us, was not just that the Dodgers were scramblers — though they certainly were that. But mainly they had that indefinable something that sports people like to call "heart".

About that same point in time — the late 1950's — a couple of mission movements were born that had a bit in common with this Dodger phenomenon. When we meet Operation Mobilization and Youth With a Mission in Chapter 8, we won't see them coming up with any grand new missionary strategies. But we will see them winning the championship in one area: recruitment. For within a decade of their foundings, these two groups began reaping the harvest of antiestablishment feelings among the young. From the viewpoint of the youth culture, these groups had "heart".

Considering my background, I could have been something less than delighted with these developments. For I had been very much a part of the "establishment" in the realm of overseas missionary activity. As an officer of Mission Aviation Fellowship, I had earlier joined other mission leaders in bemoaning the "proliferation" of new mission agencies. And as a political conservative, I had reacted like many of my peers to what was going on in the student world in the wake of the Berkeley protest movements — particularly when I saw this spreading to the Christian college campus and being reflected in the attitudes of my two older sons.

But in the end, it was these same two guys that had earlier turned me on to baseball, John and Jim, who helped me understand what their generation was feeling. Believe me, it didn't happen overnight! I did an awful lot of talking before I slowed down and began to listen. And I was only beginning to get used to these new ears when the Jesus movement surfaced in Southern California where I found myself occupying a box seat.

In the fall of 1971, when this movement was in full swing, I was meeting with a small group of mission leaders. We got together periodically for a bit of brain-storming. At this meeting, Dayton Roberts of the Latin America Mission tossed an idea at us that could be stated something like this: It seems paradoxical that as a missionary establishment we presently recruit young people from the youth culture, whom we then force to adapt to our establishmentarian standards. Then we send them out overseas to adapt once again to Third World cultures. The odd part is that our youth culture and some Third World cultures are more closely related and more similar to each other than they are to the missionary establishment.

Hmmm!

Our group decided we needed to know more about this "youth culture." We scheduled a day-long meeting that December with some of its Southern California leaders. One of these men, Don Williams (introduced in Chapter 6), brought four "street Christians" with him. After six hours of interaction, I was convinced that

Dayton's idea needed further probing. That's how the seed was planted that grew into this book.

The following spring, I was in Kabul, Afghanistan, for the annual board meeting of the International Afghan Mission. My wife and I spent a long evening at Dilaram House, a ministry to "world travelers" on the so-called "hippie trail" across Asia. And we saw a lot more of these winsome new-born Christians during the following week. My interest in these people began to take on the proportions of a love affair.

That last statement falls in a category that used to be a no-no for writers. For I just admitted my bias. Be advised, I did it on purpose. I wanted to join the growing number of writers who have undertaken to expose the myth of objectivity. Or perhaps I should say, the myth of impartiality. For I have tried to be fair, honest, even critical (in the best sense); and I hope I've avoided naiveté. But I am not neutral. You'll get more out of this book if you know, as my young friends say, where my head is — also *my* "heart".

At any rate, my admiration involved some mixed motives. For my commitment to cross-cultural missions was also an intense concern. I was even then phasing out of the organization I'd helped build, but I was sure my "second career" would still find me caught up in world missions. Why? Because I could see mounting evidence that around the world, formerly unresponsive peoples were becoming more responsive to the Christian Gospel, that many unreached peoples were now reachable. The time seemed right for a new wave of international faith-sharing that might well eclipse the highest points of missionary advance in the nineteenth century — or in the present one, for that matter. I wanted to be involved in this new wave; but I also coveted the participation of these intense, yet free-spirited young people.

This posed a question. Would new vehicles or structures be required, as implied by Dayton Roberts' observation, to channel the energy of the new youth culture into world missions? Should I commit myself to that as a presupposition; or should I keep the door open for the possible revision or restructuring of what Roberts called the missionary establishment?

I understood why he had not referred to the latter option. We had all known for several years that the image of our mission agencies had deteriorated substantially in the eyes of Christian students —

even before the Jesus movement surfaced. At Urbana 1967, the triennial Student Missionary Convention sponsored by the Inter-Varsity Christian Fellowship, a survey of the 10,000 participants had well documented this waning image. On this survey, the image of the individual missionary held up better than expected, and the structured church made a surprisingly good showing. But the mission agencies were clearly less than attractive. Furthermore, by the early 70's we had additional evidence that this bleak picture had deteriorated further. Not that the students were uninterested in service, including missionary service. It was the structures they were cool toward.

By the time I stepped out of mission administration in 1973, I wanted to look at the full picture. So I phrased the question this way: what vehicles (plural) are needed to channel the potential new missionary energy? This left the door open for both revised and new structures.

So much for the various stimuli behind this book. Now a word about how the chapters that follow developed. And, in the process, I want to introduce you to a few people. You see, this is my first book. And *now* I know that the idea of "acknowledgements" (or paying one's literary debts) is no mere routine courtesy. At least it's not for me. Others really did have strong influence on what follows. And the only logical place for me to start naming them is where most authors conclude. You know, ". . . my wife, without whose help . . ."

Yes, I must start with Claire because that's where this book started. Oh, I would have written a book in any case, and I'd have covered some of the same ground this one does. But it was she who gently nudged me into the never-to-be-forgotten experience of learning and reflecting at the School of World Mission in Pasadena — integrating and refining all that I thought I had learned in 27 years on the mission battle lines. How she overcame my activist-oriented resistance to academia — without damage to my fragile male (and glorious leader!) ego — is something I'll never cease to marvel at. But that's Claire.

As a result, I am heavily indebted to the remarkable faculty of Fuller Seminary's SWM. All of them have had substantial impact on my thinking. Yet because of the nature of my interest and research, the name of Ralph Winter will appear most frequently in the pages that follow. These references to his writings only scratch the surface of the benefit I've received from his creative thinking. After his first few lectures on the historical development of the Christian movement, I was "hooked". I had to know more about these early monastic communities, particularly the Celtic ones, that so irresistibly attracted young Irishmen despite their incredibly stark life styles and their strong disciplines. Similarly, what happened to Francis, and other sons of prosperous merchants in early thirteenth century Assisi, demanded a closer look; the similarities with Southern California suburbia of the 1970's were too remarkable to ignore. And the counter-culture movement initiated by Francis and his young friars proved to be much more than a passing fad. More amazingly, those societal drop-outs, living off the establishment, became aggressively missionary in the fullest sense, even though that did not appear to be a part of their original motivation. These insights into the potential fruitage and power of committed communities made my further library research an adventure.

Such probing of church history necessarily leads one back to the Bible. Here the creative teaching approaches of Dean Arthur Glasser (my good friend and colleague even before he became my valued mentor for this writing project) moved another of my long-neglected switches to the "on" position. I have attempted to take up his challenge of leaving my "beaten path through the Bible" (each of us has one) and take a fresh look at God's missionary purpose through his people. This goal inevitably is limited by time and space. And it is always potentially frustrated by the temptation to find only the supportive strands one is looking for. But whatever our awareness of this temptation, it is clear that topical study must start with the topic; it cannot start at Genesis 1:1 devoid of a proposition. Between these potential extremes I have sought out biblical principles and models that speak to my thesis.

Actually, we'll be seeking models right through Chapter 5 — first in the biblical record and then in church history. I stress the search-for-models nature of these early chapters because a view of history is involved here. Like most present-day Americans who have lived a half century or more, I have grown up in the midst of rapid technological progress. I didn't even stop to theorize that history was progressive; I merely assumed it. Hence I viewed history as a study which enables us to avoid the *errors* of the past.

Thanks primarily to Ralph Winter, I have come to view history much more positively: as a record of people's varied responses to the specific issues that confronted them in their time. I now realize that even what I viewed as yesterday's errors were sometimes smashing successes for a given period. What happens next (then and now) is that we institutionalize our successful responses; we defend these long after their time has passed and creative new responses are called for. And those "new" responses may actually be recycled applications of successful solutions worked out in an earlier era when people faced similar issues or problems. In other words, history is alive with recyclable options.

It is this view of history, new to me, that has sent me searching for currently-applicable models. Railroad pioneers didn't have to re-invent the wheel; they only had to adapt it to rails. Similarly, the committed community has a long history. We can build on a vast experience.

In order to apply these insights to my question, I wanted a clearer picture of the youth scene that prompted Dayton Roberts' seed-planting question. For this, I turned not only to the current literature, but also to leaders of ministries to the youth sub-culture. Both Floyd McClung (Dilaram House Ministries) and Don Williams gave significant follow-up help; and Floyd provided further encouragement simply by the quality of his relationship as my brother. Loren Cunningham of Youth With a Mission, Jack Sparks and his colleagues of Christian World Liberation Front and Jack Buckley of Covenant Circle (Berkeley, California) helped me understand their admirable movements — and the new consciousness. To this same end, L.E. Romaine, Associate Pastor of Calvary Chapel (Santa Ana, California), and several members of the staff at the Church on the Way (Van Nuys, California), gave generously of their time.

Beyond this, my research was limited to informal observations and discussions. For youth sub-culture people resist being typed or processed in any way. "I am a human being; please do not fold, mutilate or spindle." They don't carry that sign anymore, but the feeling remains. The IBM card is probably still the archtypal symbol of their quarrel with the establishment. On the other side of the coin, these young brothers and sisters in Christ exhibit an accepting openness which makes informal conversations with them a delight.

I'm deeply indebted to all those who have opened their heads, their lives and their hearts to me, both in groups and on a one-to-one basis. But I want to especially thank those 70 wonderful people with whom Claire and I shared a dorm at the Summer Institute of International Studies in 1975; they had a profound effect on the transition of this manuscript from academic thesis to printed volume.

But despite their help, this is not the kind of book that can really be "finished". Continued study and more evaluation are called for. For example, we need to follow the paths taken by the 5000 collegians who signed decision cards at Urbana 1973. Eight hundred of these young people indicated a primary commitment to cross-cultural mission work. The rest promised to actively consider such service as one of their options. The further choices and commitments these people make may convey some crucial messages. What kind of structures will they opt for — or out of?

I, for one, cannot sit by and wait for data to tabulate. My temperament is not very compatible to research (which no doubt shows clearly in this book). I prefer the enabler role. Still, we can learn a lot while enabling if we ask the right questions — and then listen. Really listen. I would be gratified if this present project stimulates and encourages others in this dual role, as it has stimulated me. And I would welcome the opportunity to share and compare findings.

CHAPTER 1

Communities of the Church

How does the word "community" grab you? What "feel" does it give you?

For many people today, it has a nostalgic ring. The idea of community suggests a more stable, less hurried time "back there" when people lived in smaller and more integrated towns or neighborhoods. That's not to say that very many 1976 people would like to pack up everything and move back to yester-year's small town with all its provincialism and gossip! But "community" seems to sift out the *good* side of those so-called good ol' days, which admittedly were both good and bad — and also just so-so.

All this suggests that for most of us, "community" has come to designate more a spirit than a place. It also suggests that it is a bit hard to come by in our kind of world — and that we miss and long for it.

So it is not surprising that Christian writers are increasingly using this term when they discuss the Church. This is hardly new. The Church has always had this ideal character and enjoyed this designation — if not the full reality. But the emphasis is particularly appropriate today; for "community" is an excellent word-picture of what the Church can and should be (I have still not said that it "is".) And this picture accords with what today's hurting world — no matter how indistinctly, or even subconsciously — is reaching out for.

In saying this, we immediately recognize that if we are going to project or focus this should-be picture of the Church-as-community

1

for these hurting people, we not only have to sharpen up the quality of our community life, but we have to do that at the *local* level. If you're going to have real community, as we've been discussing it, you have to get practical about factors like size and proximity. This is one reason why my chapter title is plural. For it is only via the know-and-be-known reality of its *many* communities that the loftier concept of *the* Church as community has any hope of being realized.

I hope no one will interpret that last paragraph as a brief for congregational polity. What we're talking about is far less ecclesiastical than social. Anthropologists like to talk about face-to-face societies. That's a good pictorial term. It focuses on the most essential ingredient for developing close personal relationships. True, even face-to-face relationships can and do go awry or stagnate. But at least there is no distortion from connecting "media"; so we at least have the *potential* for the kind of community that we find such a felt-need for in our world, and our churches — whether congregational, connectional or hierarchical.

Linkages

Now all of these ecclesiastical traditions not only have local face-to-face fellowships or communities (usually called "congregations"), but *some* form of tying these groups together. For Baptist and "free" churches, this linkage may be relatively informal and voluntary. For Roman Catholics it is quite formal, obligatory and strictly defined. We may refer to these group-to-group relationships as parishes, presbyteries or districts. And the larger groupings thus formed usually develop further linkages with names like diocese, synod and conference. These, in turn, form denominations, yearly meetings, etc.

Catholics and Anglicans refer to these linkage groups collectively as a heirarchy — a term that gives most Protestants the creeps! Yet I don't think many of us would want to go to the other extreme and define these linkages as communities. Oh, we *could*. After all, a group of European countries are linked by what they call an Economic Community. They could as well have called it a "league" (except that the toothless League of Nations pretty well scratched that term in Europe). And, after all, the word community connotes relatedness — it doesn't *have* to carry all the warm, intimate freight I've been loading onto it above. We know what those European countries mean: they've opted to *relate* their economies in a planned, defined fashion; but "brotherhood" isn't even an objective. Obviously our between-congregations links involve a closer relationship than *that*.

Yet since community, as we've been discussing it, *is* a goal within the Church, it's more important to us than it is to European statesmen that our usage be very clear. And this little exercise in "meanings" (for which words are labels — and often called on to label more than one meaning) further underscores the need of focalizing Church-as-community at the face-to-face level.

That's not to say that the linkages we've been talking about above are unimportant. Far from it! For these structures are some of the vehicles by which the comm-unity of the local groups is reflected in the comm-unity of the whole.

Structures

Now we'd better pause right here and take a close look at that word "structure" I've just used. For we could hardly discuss our present subject intelligibly without it. In fact, that word is going to be our constant companion throughout this book. You see, this is a book about structures. For communities, too, are structures.

Structure is a very broad word. It's closely related to "form". All human society has some form or structure. This may be as small and warm as a close, tightly-knit, loving family; or it may be as big and impersonal as IBM or that European Economic Community. A structure, as I plan to use the term, may have a very low profile or it may be highly visible; it may enable people, or it may pervade and control their lives; it may be planned, or it may just happen.

This is clearly a broader term than "organization". And my use of it also represents a conscious effort to avoid that alternative. As you will see later on, I'm concerned about where our American culturally-induced organizational trend has taken us. It's not that I see this as all bad; and I've tried to offer a spectrum of structural alternatives. But you'll find me leaning toward the lower profile structures — toward what we sometimes call, quite imprecisely, the "non-structured".

Now as we apply all this to the congregations and linkage groups we've been discussing, we can say of each one that it both *is* a structure and it *has* structure. (We routinely use the word both ways.) And we can say the same about a large denomination or a hierarchy. But what of the Church as a whole? Well, the visible, world-wide Church has many structures, and therefore it might not be stretching a point to say that it "has structure." But you can't say that it "is" a structure — because of its dividedness.

But suppose for a moment that those divisions could be healed. Would the Church then *be* a structure? If you're wrinkling your brow at that question, join the club. Very few of us are willing to conceive of the Church in that term. Yet few if any would deny that the Church — the Body of Christ on Earth — *has* structure. And this is true quite apart from divisions based on theological, geographic and ethnic differences. Far more importantly, it has structure that begins on the level of many local communities or fellowships, and includes various group-to-group linkage structures by which it expresses its wider comm-unity.

Other Structures

Still, these local and linkage structures do not by any means exhaust the *kinds* of structures that the Church "has". For example, there are service structures — some to serve the life of the Church (e.g. seminaries), some to serve the world (e.g. relief agencies) and some to serve both (hospitals, publishing houses, etc.). These service structures may or may not be related to one of the linkage structures (e.g. a denomination or diocese).

Now clearly these service structures are rather different, functionally, from the local fellowships. For the latter center on people: their needs and their relationships. But each service structure is built around an activity or task. That doesn't mean that the local fellowships carry out no tasks, or that the personnel of the service structures have no relationships! We're talking about the *focus* of each kind of structure. And on the basis of our comparison so far, we could say, as some have, that these foci divide the Church into "come structures" and "go structures". Let's pursue that idea.

There certainly is a come-ness about the congregational structure; for it is open to all Christians. Even if one local fellowship sets up rather strict and "exclusive" qualifications for membership, other local congregations will open the door. There's a place for every Christian believer. That includes, of course, the young — both in age and "in Christ". It also includes the stunted, the rebellious, the lazy and the complacent. And it includes those with higher desires but fearful hearts. For all of these, and others as well, the congregation is first and foremost a *nurture structure*.

So far, we've cited a second set of structures in terms of their service or task orientation. But if we'd trace some of these groups back to their origins, we'd nearly always find another crucial ingredient in the motivation of the founders. These men first and foremost wanted to serve *God*. The task that God gave them to do was important but secondary. In fact, the history we are going to review in chapters 3 and 4 will show that the "cause" or task of these structures often developed quite a bit later; many of them were originally formed by Christians who needed a vehicle for expressing their deepening relationship to God. In this sense, they are not so much "go" structures as go *on* structures — made up of those who want to go on with their God to deeper commitment.

Commitment

Yes, commitment is a key factor that separates these two kinds of structures that make up the Church. All congregations — even those that limit actual membership to persons making a personal decision and profession — find themselves faced with a universal fact: the commitment level of their people varies widely. This poses a dilemma. For on the one hand, every Christian believer, no matter how weak or lightly committed, has a right to the fellowship and caring concern of his brethren. As we've already noted, this is a primary reason for the existence of the local *nurture* structure. Yet some provision must be made for growing, highly-motivated members to express their deeper commitment. For it is through these people that the Church at large becomes dynamic. They must not only be permitted to rise above the least common denominator — this should be positively encouraged. In fact, ideally, channels for expressing this commitment ought to be provided.

Yet, as our study will show, the nurture structures down through history have been loathe to provide such channels, and slow to bless those that have emerged. In fact, they have often clawed at the heels of those members who have reached out for deeper forms of commitment. What we are talking about, of course, is frankly a form of elitism; and elitism almost inevitably produces tension. But tension is not negative, per se. It can be either creative or destructive.

Of course, this whole concept of elitism has particularly negative overtones in American society where we loudly proclaim our equalitarian convictions. The fact that much of our practice fails to square with this ideal does not eliminate the problem. For we really think we believe in equality. John W. Gardner, Chairman of Common Cause and former Secretary of Health, Education and Welfare, once wrote an important book on a related subject in the secular context: elitism in the matter of performance. He called the book *Excellence*. The sub-title asks a question: Can we be equal and excellent too? He wrestles with "the conflicting demands of excellence and equality" (Gardner 1961).* We must, in our context, wrestle with the conflicting demands of *commitment* and equality.

Committed Christians through history have sought a solution to this struggle. Characteristically (but not exclusively) they did this in the company of similarly-committed Christian brothers and sisters. In doing so, they developed a host of structures (to which we shall devote the next four chapters) that relatively few Protestants think of as "Church". This is not surprising. For the leadership of the nurture structures (congregations *and* linkage structures) on whom we largely depend for our Christian education have always tended to a mono-structural view of the Church. In fact, our theologians tend to *define* the Church in terms of this nurture structure.

Two Structures

Recognizing this bias, Ralph Winter (who first introduced me to the two-structure concept) prefers to speak in terms of the two structures of God's "redemptive mission." He points out that the nurture structure, when it emerged in the first century, could have been appropriately described as a "Christian synagogue." Later, when it became patterned on Roman political forms, it was termed

---

* Throughout this book, when I quote another author or make a reference to his work, I will give his name and the year of his work. One or both will usually be in parenthesis. By this code you can immediately identify that item in the Bibliography at the end of this volume. Sometimes I will refer to specific page numbers — separated from the date by a colon.

"parish" and "diocesan". Today we may call it "local church", "synodical" or "diocesan", depending on our view of polity. Winter often uses a specialized term, "modality", to refer to this synagogue/parish/diocesan structure (Winter 1974).

"Sodality", Winter's chosen term for the *other* structure, is frequently used in Catholic circles (and occasionally by Baptist historian Kenneth Latourette) to describe a church-related (some would say "para-ecclesiastical") *society*. Dictionary and anthropological definitions support this usage: a fellowship, a fraternity, a brotherhood. Winter pours additional meaning into his use of the term, centering around the theme of commitment. Thus a Christian sodality, the second structure of the Church which we shall be examining in some biblical and historical detail, is made up of committed Christians who have made an "adult second decision" beyond deciding for Christ and joining a local fellowship of believers *(ibid:127)*. That decision involves an above-average expression of their Christian faith: a commitment to a life-style and/or a ministry beyond the norms of the local gathered fellowship. I shall be using this term "sodality" in this way with some frequency. It becomes a useful synonym for my use of "committed community."

On the other hand, I will use Winter's coined term, "modality", sparingly. Many people apparently find this matched pair of unfamiliar terms confusing — like stalactite and stalagmite. In its place I shall sometimes use "churchly structure(s)" (though I recognize the inconsistency, since it is my thesis that the two structures together constitute the Church). More often I will use "nurture structure(s)" or simply "congregation(s)".

So much for the definitions.

Now we're going to take a tour of the models. As your tour director, I wanted you to know what *kind* of models we're looking for and why. The "why" will become even clearer as we move through the tour.

The first stop is the Bible. Familiar ground? Maybe you'd better wait and answer that later.

CHAPTER 2

Committed Bands

Where do you start looking for models of the Church in the Bible? Why, in Acts, of course!

Nothing in the previous 88.5% of the text? What about that "church in the wilderness" that we read about in Acts 7:38 (AV)? Now *there* was a group of people in need of nurture! (And yet they were, by God's gracious choice, the People of God!) They don't exactly dazzle us with their outreach orientation — or even their commitment. Are we apt to find models of the sodality, the committed elite, amidst this often-massive nominalism? There are, to be sure, very committed individuals. But what about groups? Well, this is part of the tour, so let's check it out.

I should warn you, though: the roads in this back country are rather neglected. There are stretches of asphalt in Genesis and Isaiah; and most of the Psalms are paved. But there's no real Interstate until you get to Matthew. That's just the way it is today. Nevertheless, I found the old back roads fascinating — makes me want to explore them some more. Maybe you'll feel the same.

Anticipations

As somewhat expected, I found the Old Testament sodality models more implicit than explicit. And even then, some are given such passing reference that they barely escape obscurity.

At first glance, Genesis seems to focus only on key individuals. One might even say that whenever men in patriarchal society joined together for a task, their goals were totally wrong. So it was at Babel.

And so it was when most of Joseph's brothers conspired to sell him into Egyptian slavery — hardly the ideal type of commissioning service for a cross-cultural missionary!

On the other hand, we picture faithful Noah standing alone against the tide. We aren't told how committed his sons were — whether they were a part of the ship-building project or only on the passenger list. This is the way stories are told in a patriarchal society. Noah may have headed a reasonably committed family sodality. We just don't know.

We'd hardly look for a sodality, strictly defined, during Israel's 40-year wilderness experience. Getting them to stick with a *first* decision to be the people of God was a mammoth enough task. But we do see greater degrees of commitment emerging from time to time. Witness the minority report of Joshua and Caleb when they were part of a covert intelligence-gathering mission into Palestine. Joshua followed this up, years later, with his classic declaration in Joshua 24:15. ". . . as for me and my house, we will serve the LORD."* This solidarity of the patriarchal family may be viewed as an early group expression of commitment.

The period of the judges seems even more fragmented, and individualistic, when "every man did what was right in his own eyes" (17:6, 21:25). Joint enterprises were principally for defense, a periodic necessity. Here again, the individual leader-heroes hold center stage, though we see some aspects of the small, committed sodality foreshadowed in Gideon's select band. We note from the symbolism of how the men quenched their thirst, that God's "regulars" tend to be irregular, or even non-conformist, by human standards. This later becomes more explicit in the "Do not be conformed . . ." of Romans 12:1,2.

As the children of Israel chose to become the kingdom of Israel we read of two prominent young men who remind us a bit of the sons of the wealthy at Assisi, Italy, twenty-two centuries later. However, neither David nor Jonathan was as free as Francis. For a time, David had his band which Jonathan could not join. But survival, not service, was the focus of these refugees. A high sense of brotherhood was smothered by the intrigues of kingdom that Samuel had specifically warned the people about.

* Scripture quotations are from the Revised Standard Version unless otherwise noted.

Prophetic Brotherhoods

With the coming of the prophets, we begin to see a stronger type of second-decision commitment to a God-appointed role. Again, if we look only on the surface, it would appear that each of these courageous men walked his unpopular road alone. But here and there we catch a glimpse of a special group that related to at least some of these risk-taking spokesmen for God. One such group appears under Samuel's apparent leadership when the prophetic tradition was still in its infancy. They're referred to in I Samuel 10:10 as a "band of prophets" and in 19:20 as "the company of the prophets."

A seemingly similar group appears in the early chapters of II Kings as Elijah's task falls to Elisha — including the leadership of these "sons of the prophets" (2:3 to 4:44). The role and scope of this group must depend largely on conjecture, though we note that approximately 100 of them met at Gilgal on one occasion (II Kings 4:43 and context). Much later, we get one final glimpse of this movement. When Amos declares that he was called from outside the prophetic tradition, he may be saying that he was not "one of the sons of the prophets" (Amos 7:14, margin). The Jerusalem Bible fully supports this alternate reading: ". . . neither did I belong to any of the brotherhoods of the prophets." This suggests that one or more such sodality structures might have existed for more than 300 years, from the establishment of the kingdom until the exile.

Even during the exile we see a Franciscan-like sense of brotherhood existing between Daniel and his three friends. Was this bond of mutual support a part of the reason why they stood so staunchly for God's honor in the face of such opposition?

The Remnant and the Proselytizers

Before leaving the Old Testament record, we should pause just a moment to examine a concept (in contrast to the live people and concrete events already cited) that bears on our subject: the prophets frequent reference to a remnant (e.g. Amos 3:12, 4:11; Isaiah 1:9). We don't have to read far into the historical books before we're aware that the people of God are not, after all, synonymous with the citizens of Israel. This is illustrated forcefully when Jehovah advises Elijah (following his encounter with the Baal cult on Mt. Carmel) of 7000 faithful though secret followers. It is illustrated further by those who returned from exile to rebuild Jerusalem (and thus laid the physical groundwork for Messiah's coming). These constituted a remnant from among the much larger number who chose to remain in Babylon because, Josephus says, they were not willing to leave their possessions. Certainly many of the latter loved and worshipped Jehovah. But they lacked the second-decision commitment of the returnees who were willing to accept pioneering conditions to carry out the purposes of God. Jerusalem was, after all, a pile of rubble.

We should also look briefly at the period between the Testaments. Blauw, in examining *The Missionary Nature of the Church,* devotes a brief chapter (he calls it an intermezzo to his biblical study) to the meager but fascinating data on the belated initiation of missionary activity among the Jews: the proselytizing movement. "It seems to me that this has been underestimated rather than overestimated with regard to its extent and intensity as well as to its significance for the missionary attitude and activity of the Christian Church in the first few centuries of its existence" (1962:55). Blauw doesn't feel it can properly be said that the diaspora itself explains Jewish missionary propaganda, though he agrees that the diaspora was its prime mover. Neither he nor De Ridder (1975:120-127) speculate on the structure of the movement. Winter does.

> Very few Christians, casually reading the New Testament, and with only the New Testament available to them, would surmise the degree to which there had been Jewish evangelists who went before Paul all over the Empire, people whom Jesus himself described as traversing land and sea to make a single proselyte. Paul followed their path . . . While we know very little about the structure of [this] evangelistic outreach within which pre-Pauline Jewish proselytizers worked . . . it would be surprising if Paul didn't follow somewhat the same procedures (1974:121,122).

This leaves a lot to conjecture. After all, Paul was a towering, creative historical figure by any standard. And the Holy Spirit could guide him either through historical precedents or in fresh, innovative paths. Here, with Blauw, we must leave this tantalizing intermezzo and return to the clear biblical record.

Acts: The Expansion Begins

Now we are ready to turn to the Acts of the Apostles which deals specifically with early church history. Roland Allen points out, however, that Luke is not concerned with overall church history; he limits his selection almost exclusively to those events which have some important bearing upon the preaching of the Gospel to those outside the Church (Allen 1972:13). This missionary tone is established at the outset by the Lord's final statement of the Great Commission (1:8) which spells out three phases or levels of proclamation, and forms a 3-point outline for the book. Geographically stated, this was to involve local (Jerusalem), provincial (Judea/Samaria) and world-wide evangelism.

Let's look at those three historical phases in terms of how the evangelistic efforts of the early Church were structured, with an emphasis on phase three where we see the greatest degree of on-purpose effort and planning.

Over-viewing the first six chapters of Acts, the life of the young Jerusalem church seems best summed up in the words: community and witness. These early Christians were deeply involved *together*. They cared for one another and supported each other through high times (chapters 2-4), low times (chapter 5) and times of disagreement (6:1-7). The several references to the growth of the church during this period (2:47, 4:4, 4:33, 5:12-14, 6:7) suggest that the life of the community was so attractive that it played a strong role, along with the preaching, in winning believers. We have here a beautiful picture of a local or city-wide church in its first love, radiating Christ's love through its community life, its worship and its spontaneous verbal witness. However, no indication yet of a plan to carry the message beyond the city limits.

Phase 2 began abruptly — with the martyrdom of Stephen. "On that day a great persecution arose against the church in Jerusalem, and they were all scattered throughout the region of Judea and Samaria except the apostles" (8:1). The "all" of this verse may have had most specific reference to the Hellenists or Greek-speaking Jews (Barker 1969:134-141). For we see Saul in verse 3 finding ample local residents to imprison as a result of his house to house searches. At any rate, we should not be too surprised to find that these earliest missionaries, or sent-ones, were "sent" by persecution. A careful study of history, dating clear back to Naaman's slave girl (II Kings 5:1-19), reveals a tremendous amount of missionary activity carried out as a result of unintended mobility. God gives us the privilege of willing choice. But he hasn't limited himself to our weak hearing or our slow feet. So it was with phase 2, beginning with Acts 8. Crisis created the mobility.

What about the structure of *these* mission efforts. At first glance, it all appears pretty individualistic — quite the opposite of the Jerusalem community. Philip, the most prominent evangelist, may have had close colleagues, but there's no mention of them. (He was joined temporarily by Peter and John in one of his successes.) Many of the scattered Hellinists may have gone to the homes of relatives, and evangelized across what Dr. Donald McGavran calls the "bridges" of God, i.e. kinship ties (1955). More certainly, they would have scattered in groups (probably family groups) rather than as individuals. But all this we must surmise. What we are specifically told is that churches sprang up and developed throughout area 2 (9:31).

There is some ambiguity as to where phase 3 begins. Philip was led of the Spirit (on a seemingly solo mission) to share the Gospel with a prominent member of the Ethiopian court (8:26-40) — though most historians find no evidence of a church there prior to the fourth century. Peter, taking a small band of brothers with him, opened the door of faith to the gentiles on specific instructions from the Spirit (chapter 10). Meanwhile, the same thing happened on a less dramatic scale at a place called Antioch (11:19-24). And it was from here that, structurally speaking, phase three really got underway.

The Missionary Bands

The selection of the first recorded on-purpose missionary band is recounted in the first several verses of Acts 13 (JB). ". . . the Holy Spirit said, 'I want Barnabas and Saul set apart for the work to which I have called them.' . . . So these two . . . went . . ." While only the two are mentioned here in verses 2 and 4, we find John (Mark) mentioned in verse 5 and there's a reference to "friends" in verse 13. The team or band may still have been quite small, but it was clearly more than a pair. Interestingly, from verse 13 onward, Paul's name appears first whenever the two are mentioned. Apparently Barnabas deferred to the growing development of Paul's leadership gift. This no doubt required a good deal of grace, but it probably also gave Barnabas a lot of satisfaction. After all, he actively believed in Paul when the others in Jerusalem were still a bit fearful (9:27). Then as a missionary to the growing fellowship of believers at Antioch, Barnabas again reached out for the man he believed in, and sought out Paul to join the leadership team there (11:25-26).

In the light of this seemingly-ideal relationship, we can't help but feel sad about that "violent quarrel" which separated them (15:36-40, JB). And yet, there may be important reasons for this — well beyond the matter of the "old man" periodically asserting itself in spiritual leaders, just as in other Christians. In the first place, there was a big job to do. It certainly could not be done by one team; it would take many teams. And to assure good leadership, the best growth would be by division. Yet who wants to divide a beautifully-functioning community voluntarily?

But more than quantity was involved. By the Creator's design, no two people are fully alike. Societal groupings and structures (family, clan, village, culture) consciously or unconsciously provide for this diversity. But highly-committed communities, particularly those focused on a task, need a greater degree of commonality. Consequently, to absorb all the committed energy, some diverse options must be available. Barnabas, the "son of encouragement" (4:36), could continue to spot the potential missionary leaders and patiently develop them in on-the-job opportunities, as he had done with Paul. Because of this enabling ministry, Barnabas' next protege (his nephew, John Mark) would one day be "useful" to Paul (II Tim. 4:11). But for now, Paul needed team mates who could happily mesh with the shape-up-or-ship-out style of his leadership at that time.

At any rate, the first missionary band had accomplished its purpose. It had demonstrated the powerful utility and effectiveness of a small, tightly-knit, task-oriented community. The time had come to multiply these bands.

You can't help but wonder how many more times this happened in the first century alone. You wish you could peek behind the curtain and see many other teams forming. Maybe we do get a glimpse of this in passages like II Timothy 2:9-12. Tychicus was "sent" out with Paul's blessing: Crescens and Titus have "gone"; no indication of why. What about Demas? We can certainly sympathize with Paul's feelings. But maybe — just maybe — Demas was showing only a bit more of the "old man" than Paul and Barnabas did back in Acts 15. Maybe once again God was getting Demas split off for leadership of a different kind of missionary band. Is it even possible that Paul was in prison so that additional leadership would emerge more quickly? *Well!*

At any rate, we note some interesting things about these bands. For one thing, they weren't static or inflexible; team composition was in flux. Luke was in-and-out of Paul's team. So, apparently were Timothy, Titus, and John Mark. There apparently was communication and fellowship between teams even when they were going separate ways.

Another interesting feature is that these teams are never described in a didactic way. Yet the abundant evidence of their activity shows how thoroughly they were accepted as a valid and vital structure of the Church, the Body of Christ. But is it really so strange that Paul, who was responsible for so much of the New Testament's formal teaching, would not *describe* the missionary band? After all, he was *demonstrating* its function at every step. And he also demonstrated his relationship to the local nurturing fellowships that he and his teams planted — by the way he wrote to these congregations in certain cities. We catch even further revealing insights about this relationship when Paul writes to his sometime teammates, Timothy and Titus, who are then involved in the selection and encouragement of local leadership within these planted fellowships (e.g. Titus 1:5).

The Bands and the Local Fellowships

On the other hand, the Scriptural material is extremely skimpy regarding the connection between the missionary bands and any "originating" or "sending" fellowships. We'd be on shaky ground to place the Jerusalem church in such a category. Their principal linkage with the missionary bands seems to be an endless asking of nit-picking doctrinal questions (Acts 11:2,3; 15:1,5 etc.). This tendency became so strong that it once caused Peter to sacrifice his principles (Gal. 2:12,13). (I imagine that every mission leader reading this will get an immediate mental picture of one or more constituency churches that he feels threatened by!) This trend continued to the point where James and the elders had to warn Paul, when he arrived in Jerusalem for his last visit, about the thousands of Jewish believers there, "all zealous for the law," who had believed some distorted rumors about his attitude toward the law.

Here was a drift into cultural Christianity so strong that it took precedence over Christian charity and brotherhood. And judging by the advice the elders gave Paul, they were powerless to counteract the trend (Acts 21:20-26). What a tragic contrast with the high community and spontaneous witness of chapters 2 through 6. The growingly inbred, law-fencing Jerusalem church is hardly a model of a mission-minded church possessing a universal message for all mankind.

The cosmopolitan church at Antioch is, of course, quite another story. And it's from this one example that we tend to draw most of our present thinking about "the sending church." Yet here again, we really have very little to go on. We know that the first two missionary leaders were a part of the leadership band of the young church. (Both were outsiders brought in to strengthen the leadership — probably only temporarily.) The Holy Spirit chose this time, place and group of men to initiate the first missionary band. As a result, Paul and Barnabas certainly had warm feelings of affection and collegiality with this group. They apparently delighted to share reports of their successes with them. But there is no evidence that the life of the missionary band was "rooted" in or controlled by this church. Nor is there any hint of a financial supportive relationship.

On the contrary, the evidence points to the fact that the bands had a life of their own, and threw off shoots which became the planted communities of believers. Green (following Harnack) calls attention to this distinction as it carried over into the second century. (Though he is writing in the context of ministries rather than structures, per se.) He speaks of a division of "peripatetic Christian leaders which was extremely ancient, and probably modeled on Jewish precedent; they stand out in sharp contrast to the settled ministry of bishops, presbyters and deacons . . . Both types of ministry are found side by side in the *Didache* and Hermas . . . The roving ministry were . . . not elected by the churches, like the settled ministry" (Green 1970:168).

We have here a clearly autonomous structure. But autonomy does not mean independence or separate existence. Without interdependence between the bone structure and the muscular structure there would be no human body. Glasser speaks of the sodality in Acts "within and between congregations. Paul and his band were a disciplined, mobile group that performed an evangelistic, church-planting function." One purpose of his letter to the Church at Rome was to draw "it into his forthcoming mission to Spain (Romans 1:5; 15:24)" (Glasser 1973:62,63).

The total picture is one of partnership: a horizontal relationship, not a vertical one. *Yes!*

Now, looking back, we've found little bands of the more fully committed scattered through the biblical history. At first, it seems, these communities served a primarily faith-preserving function — particularly in times of wide-spread nominalism and apostasy. But after the exile, we see a growing trend for the commitment of these second-decision people to be expressed in a task or a mission (rebuilding Jerusalem, the proselytizing movement). Finally, in the young church we see the primary focus of the sodality centered on the missionary mandate.

The scanty historical records of the early Christian centuries tell us a lot less than we'd like to know about what happened next. It would be nice to know what effect persecution had on these early sodalities — and how church leaders handled the inevitable tensions that develop between the two basic structures. We won't waste time speculating. We're not trying to "cover" Church history in any event. We're intentionally selecting the clearest models — the ones that might be most helpful to us today.

So we need now to move on to the first clear revival of the sodality idea. At least it's the first that we know of. This arose out of the nominalism that accompanied the onset of the Constantinian period. With Nathanael, you may want to ask, "Can anything good come out of the Constantinian period?" I can understand that. But with Philip, let me just say, "Come and see."

CHAPTER 3

Monks and Friars

Ralph Winter is so right: any reference to monasteries gives Protestants culture shock! But there's no way we can discuss committed communities in church history, while sidestepping the models we find in the monastic and mendicant orders. So let's see if we can establish some kind of rapport with this historical and ecclesiastical phenomena.

Maybe we should approach this via the back door. Let's look at our attitude toward *another* historical model: what we often call "the New Testament Church." Here's an outstanding exception to our normally "progressive" view of history. We are inclined to view this model not only admiringly, but as an ultimate, if not flawless, ideal. For a nostalgic moment we aren't thinking about that troublesome church at Corinth with its strong party spirit and assorted sinners, including at least one case of unabashed incest. Nor do we have in immediate view those wretched roaming judaizers (who, after all were impliedly believers, no matter how immature); or those at Galatia and Corinth who were so easily taken in by them. And most certainly of all, we are excluding some of those churches John addresses in Revelation 2 and 3.

Why this one-sided attitude? Well, we're just human, that's all. It's always easier and more comfortable to collect things neatly into categories, labeling some good and some bad. In time, we just ignore what we knew at the outset: that even the best are a mixture. By parable, Christ reminded us that this fact of life is particularly

18

applicable to his Kingdom because of the spiritual battle Satan is constantly waging. He chose two agricultural labels: wheat and tares. In his parable, there were tares among the wheat. In other cases we might find only some wheat among the tares. But the point is: we shouldn't fall into the trap of simplistically labeling fields wheat or tares by the predominant growth. For if we do, we're going to miss some important historical lessons.

And so it is with the monks and the monasteries. On the one hand, the original movement certainly did involve, for some, a flee-the-world mentality — a concentration on their own salvation with seemingly little concern for the eternal destiny of others. And theologically, some of the Catholic concepts that trouble Protestants so much were perpetuated in the monastic movement: earning salvation by spiritual works, the evil nature of flesh and matter, and legalism in general.

On the other hand, as Baptist historian, Kenneth Scott Latourette points out, the movement was (negatively) a reaction against a growing laxity within the Church and (positively) a reaching out for the ideals in the teachings of Jesus and the apostles. These characteristics of the movement were winsomely attractive. "Hundreds of monks, including the most famous of the pioneers, gave spiritual counsel to those who came to them" (1953:221-223). Latourette also calls attention to other renewal and reformation characteristics of the movement that appear repeatedly in the subsequent seventeen centuries.

> At first it was primarily a lay movement, not within the hierarchical structure of the clergy. To some degree it was a rebellion of the individual against the organization of the Catholic Church, regimented as that was under the bishops and clergy. Indeed, at times its members were quite unsubmissive to the bishops and were insubordinate, even tumultuously so, against a particular bishop (ibid.).

Maybe that will help us, as American Protestants, to identify with the movement a bit better!

Monastic Movements

Now let's take a small step backward, time-wise, and note how the early churches developed structurally. In a few well-phrased sentences, Latourette traces the almost-inevitable trend toward the particular committed communities we are examining at the moment.

> From the very start, Christians, instead of attempting to transform all society . . . formed themselves into groups more or less distinct from the world . . . As larger numbers came into the Church and the descendants of converts remained in it, Christians tended to conform more and more to the social order in which they were set. Against this, as we have said, came protests in the form of efforts to organize communities which would live according to the precepts of Jesus and the apostles. Of these the monastic movement was the most widespread and the most persistent (1970a:354).

To be sure, not all of monasticism expressed itself in community. There were the individualistic hermits, too. But the idea of a community, under *regula* or rule, became the dominant characteristic of the movement. And these communities became the principal committed alternative to the nominal kind of Christianity so often found in the diocesan churches where eventually membership was almost synonymous with citizenship.

At least this was the picture in the Roman Catholic and Eastern Churches as the movement spread from Egypt, Palestine, and Asia Minor westward to Gaul and other parts of Europe. But very early, a monastic movement developed further westward in Ireland that produced some very distinctive forms. In the first place, it tended to eclipse the concept of the diocese. For the latter, after all, was very much a Roman concept and the Romans had never crossed over to Ireland. Furthermore, a diocese was organized with a town of some political importance as its center, and Ireland had no such towns. As a result, Irish Christianity developed what McNeill calls a "strange inversion of jurisdictions" in which the church "was under the leadership of abbots who were secondarily bishops, or had bishops attached to their monasteries and under their jurisdiction" (1974:69,70).

As noted above, the tribal and rural character of Irish society no doubt played a significant part in this pattern. Yet it is not as though such a structure was forced on the people. On the contrary, many of the founders of the Irish monasteries, like their Egyptian counterparts, originally sought a retreat in some remote spot with a few companions. But, as McNeill says, "They found themselves pursued by throngs of young men eager to follow their example and to obey their rules . . . It is possible that in Ireland a larger percentage of the whole population than anywhere else entered monastic communities. Nowhere else in Christendom was the culture of a people so completely embraced within monasticism" (*ibid:*70).

Now here is a model that clearly deserves a closer look — a segment of the Church where the committed communities represented more than the usual small vanguard. And thanks to a recent surge of interest in Celtic studies, we now know a good deal more about the distinctives of Irish Christianity, including its tremendous participation (all out of proportion to the small population involved) in the evangelization of Europe. We'll try not to ignore the Eastern and Roman monasteries, for we'll find useful patterns of commitment, community and mobility there also. But through the first Christian millenium, we'll inevitably identify best with the Irish.

Irish Distinctives

As we've already implied, one reason for the vitality of Irish Christianity was its indigeneity; it took root in the native soil; it was "at home" in Celtic culture. This was most visible in the nature and productivity of the monasteries. We've already noted how the young were attracted to these communities. Why? McNeill says, "The Irish Christian youth felt with peculiar force the urge to ascetic devotion, and the busy life of the monasteries offered an outlet to native talent and energy in art and learning" (*ibid:*70,71).

And that ascetic devotion ought to be spelled with capital letters! The austere and seemingly-unrelaxed devotional life reflected in the Celtic Penitentials (which somewhat served the purposes of the *regula* of the Roman orders), represents an aspect of monasticism which we today have the hardest time understanding. In fact, this is one of our principal stereotypes of the early monks of the Egyptian desert; and the Irish seem, in some ways, to have outdone the Egyptian prototypes in this department! All we can say in their defense is that it apparently was a *relevant* form of expressing commitment. After all, there was that "astonishing flow of youth into the monastic life" which McNeill speaks of as the feature which most arrests our attention as we study the movement. And this attraction of young men was similarly the experience of Anthony in Egypt and Martin in Gaul *(ibid;* see also McNeill 1965).

But in Ireland that was only one side of the coin. The Irish were great lovers of art and learning, and as noted in the quotation above, this was very much a part of the life of the monastery. Along with the severe devotional exercises we see a robust enjoyment of life that is less apparent in the movement on the continent. Music was one important expression of this zest for life, but it took other artistic forms as well. This synthesis of personal fulfillment and ultimate commitment may provide a key to understanding the enduring vitality of this movement for six centuries — as well as conveying some important messages to us today.

We can most easily identify with these early Irish Christians when we find historians referring to the Celtic culture as individualistic. In fact, it is this native characteristic which contributed so much to their centuries-long non-conforming stance vis-a-vis the Roman Catholic hierarchy. This was not a matter of rejecting a vital connection with Rome; rather the Irish simply felt no need to be subservient. They had "accepted the gospel as an independent people and they maintained that independence as long as they could" (Cook 1971:48).

Yet in the midst of this cultural individualism, we also find the strongest Christian collectivism developing — as well as the greatest profusion of such communities (i.e. the monastic houses). Furthermore, we see many of these linked together in confederations that provided for growth, without diluting, by excessive size, the closeness and distinctive character of each individual community. This linking structure had a very low profile. But it was an innovative, effective way of combining Irish individualism and creativity with the strength of committed communities.

Missionary Monks

Kathleen Hughes sees this confederational structure as one of two natural foundations on which the Irish communities built their most enduring monument: the missionary conquest of Europe. "The monastic *paruchia* (confederation) had great powers of expansion:

however far the monks traveled, they were still part of the family" (1966:78). And since the monks traveled in small missionary bands, they had the felt support of two communities: their immediate colleagues and their monastic house in the Emerald Isle to which, because of their total commitment, they seldom returned.

The other natural or cultural base for missionary activity was "the desire for wandering which was still alive in a people who had been, within tribal memory, on the move" (ibid.). This was put to abundant use.

> For more than half a millennium a stream of educated and dedicated men poured from the monasteries of Ireland to "go to pilgrimage for Christ" wherever they might feel themselves divinely led . . . They were not conscripted or appointed by their superiors . . . They would obtain the consent of their abbots and start out eagerly . . . We do not read of inner crises of decision; rather we get the impression of prompt and unhesitating response to a divine imperative (McNeill 1974:155).

In his succeeding chapter, McNeill credits the Celts (and primarily the Irish) with largely evangelizing the Germanic world. They penetrated as far south as northern Italy and eastward into Slavic lands. Here also their missionary communities proved irresistably attractive. "The penalty of holiness was popularity. Men thronged in to join the devoted band . . . They rapidly enlisted Frankish and other German youth who, working harmoniously with them, made Christianity indigenous and self-perpetuating" (ibid:159,175).

I promised earlier that I would not let my enthusiasm for the Irish obscure the development of the monastic movement in the countries around the Mediterranean. As we've already noted, this involved something more than mystically-inclined social drop-outs. The persistence of the movement (despite periodic lapses) must, after all, say something about its vitality. When I make the effort to look past my Protestant biases, I have to agree with Catholic charismatic lay leader, Stephen Clark, that the early monastic (or, as he prefers to call it, "ascetic") movement was essentially a *renewal* movement. In his recent book (1976) dealing with this early movement (which he dates from 305 to 451 A.D.), he points out that all renewal movements "touch, especially in their early stages, only some Christians" (p. 3). He acknowledges the "elitism" involved, and speaks to the need for structures with "an authority of their own [that are also] related to the authority structures of the wider Church in some ongoing way" (p. 5).

> As renewal movements have appeared and grown, the people involved have collected to form communities within the Church where they could live a life permeated by the movement's ideals — renewal communities . . . It seems to be almost a sociological law: renewal movements produce renewal communities (p. 4).

Later, Clark observes that "like most renewal movements, the ascetic movement also produced a great missionary effort" (p. 67). On his next three pages he provides a catalogue of that effort. We might not identify with *all* their activities as authentic missionary work. Neither does Clark. He recognizes in an end note that *some* of their effort centered on the destruction of paganism — sort of a forerunner of the Crusade mentality. But that should not obscure the fact that some truly spiritual efforts were also involved.

As we've noted, the monastic movement periodically fell on hard times. And the hardest of those hard times was the so-called Dark Ages. Personally, I prefer Latourette's term, "The Great Recession" — despite its currently negative economic connotations. And it is Baptist Latourette who titles a chapter about the ensuing period of Church history, "Revival through Monasticism: the Rich and Varied Development of the Monastic Ideal in Western Europe" (1953:416ff.). After 950 A.D. there were recurring monastic renewal movements, sometimes within the established orders, but more often through the proliferation of new communities. In all this, the Cluny movement led the way — and basically held that leadership for two and a half centuries. The movement attracted so many youth that additional, affiliated houses were founded, making this the first "family" of monasteries.

As Cluny eventually declined through institutional obesity, "Other and younger movements took its place as pioneers. Chief of these were the Cistercians" (*ibid:*423). The Cistercians further developed the idea of welding its houses together as an integrated order, but still gave each house a large degree of autonomy. The most famous abbot of this order was Bernard, who was put in charge of its fourth, newly-opened house at Clairvaux — at the age of 25! (*ibid:*424). Cluny, the Cistercians and a host of smaller communities in the same period became renewing pre-cursors of a movement that mission-minded Protestants can more easily identify with.

Enter the Friars

Early in the thirteenth century, a whole new breed of order appeared. The members were not known as monks but as friars. While not lacking in disciplined devotion, their primary emphasis was on service. And because so many of the monastic orders had become wealthy and static, the new emphasis was on simplicity and mobility. Here was a whole new wave of committed communities in which on-purpose missionary activity was a primary focus.

The largest and best known of these are, of course, the Franciscans and the Dominicans. Because of limited space, and because it suits our purpose best, we'll deal primarily with the former.

Latourette speaks of Francis of Assisi as "one of the most winsome figures of Christian history" (ibid:429). And it is not surprising that Hollywood chose to put his community-founding years on celluloid* in the early 1970's; the parallels between the young men of Assisi and some of the idealists of the recent hippie movement are striking. Francis and his friends were disillusioned with a deteriorated war cause. They rejected the play-boy life they had once enjoyed as sons of the newly-rich mercantile class, and identified rather with the exploited poor. As beggars by choice, they too, could have been accused of living off the affluence they rejected. And finally, we see a reflection of the American church's early reaction to the Jesus movement in Erikson's observation: "In outward appearance and in their way of life, they were fellow travelers of other, heretical reformers of their time" (1970:46).

This alternative way of life was, as with other committed communities through the centuries, the foundation of the movement. It was both renewing force and non-verbal protest. Most importantly to our thesis concerning the two-structure nature of the Church, Francis' chosen life-style emphasis enabled him to obey his vision within a context of loyalty to the whole Church, deficient as the hierarchical structure was at that time.

---

* The film's title, *Brother Sun, Sister Moon* is taken from Francis' most famous devotional poem, "Canticle of Brother Sun."

Saint Francis neither openly criticized the established order of the Church for its pomp and vainglory nor for the prevalent depravity of the clergy. By consistently maintaining standards of simplicity and devotion in his own life, he highlighted these deficiencies and silently focused attention on them. It was characteristic of him that he avoided challenging the authority of the Church and demanded of his brothers that all priests be treated with deep respect. He also invariably turned to the highest authority available for guidance and sanction. He early sought out the Bishop of Assisi, then Pope Innocent III, and finally Cardinal Ugolino. In personal confrontation he won the trust and respect of these high dignitaries and then serenely proceeded on his own idiosyncratic way *(ibid:47)*.

The Franciscan commitment to "life style" is strongly reflected in the *Regula,* or Rule, of the order. The opening sentence begins, "1. This is the Rule and way of life of the brothers minor;" and the next paragraph starts, "2. If any wish to adopt this way of life . . . (Bettenson 1967:128,129). Clearly, the order was more a way of life than an organization — at least at the outset. The emphasis on their relationship to one another as *brothers* is also strongly reflected in the Rule.

Once again, the result was popularity and attraction, which now included not only young men, but young women and, later, married people of all ages. Within three years of his first commitment, Francis received young Clare into the order, leading to the founding of the auxiliary Poor Ladies or Poor Clares. The relationship of this "second order" to the friars was not only auxiliary but complementary. Here was an early, probably unconscious, attempt to re-introduce the wholeness of male/female contribution to the celibate orders. The Poor Clares represented a stability that complemented the activities of the wandering friars. And the latter served as providers for the women who did not participate in the begging.

The "third order", or Order of Penitents, was also formed very early.

Its members were not fully to follow the way of Francis and were to remain in the world and hold property, but they were to be sparing in food and drink, give alms, abstain from vice, accept the sacraments, and remain loyal members of the Catholic Church (Latourette 1953:432).

The committed community was becoming multi-form and multi-level. And the renewing effect on the Church at large was significant.

The effect on missionary outreach was even more pronounced. As we've already noted, this was a primary and on-purpose activity of the friars. The revised rule of St. Francis reflects the voluntarism, the communal involvement, and the objective screening involved in the sending out of missionaries.

> Whoever of the brothers *by divine inspiration* may wish to go among the Saracens and other infidels, shall *seek permission* to do so from their provincial ministers. But to none shall the ministers give permission to go, save to those whom they shall see to be *fit* for the mission (Bettenson 1967:132, emphasis is mine).

Hundreds of the brothers passed through this grid, and "Before the thirteenth century is out, we shall find Franciscans at the ends of the known earth" (Neill 1964:117). This includes the famous encountering of the new Khan at Cambaluc (Peking) by John of Monte Corvino in 1294. And with the onset of the Age of Discovery, later Franciscans took ship to even wider horizons.

We should note that the contemporary Dominicans were equally missionary in purpose, as reflected in the name of the society within their order: The Company of Brethren Dwelling in Foreign Parts among the Heathen for the Sake of Christ. We should also note a basic and fundamental difference between these two counter-cultural orders. Neill draws the contrast via the aims of the founders who were contemporaries.

> Francis lived to bring back simplicity and joy into the Christian world, and to release new forces for the service of the very poor. In the work of Dominic there were from the beginning harsher traits. His Order was to be intellectually competent, devoted to the conversion of heretics particularly through the work of preaching, as its official title the "Order of Preachers" indicates (Neill 1964:116).

There is every evidence that the complementary roles of these two largest orders were both very much needed at that juncture of history. And they were supplemented by a host of smaller brotherhoods. This multiple response to diverse needs once again calls forth the genius of the sodality concept.

We could take one further chronological step in the history of Catholic orders and deal with the most extensive missionary effort of them all, the Society of Jesus. But the word "Jesuit" waves the most crimson of red flags in the face of Protestants. For the often-admirable missionary activities of the Jesuits among unbelievers, tends to be occluded by their zealous, often excessive efforts to reconvert Protestants. Furthermore, we have spent long enough on the celibate community models. We must soon move on to those involving families.

But first we should review these first 1500 years of church history in terms of two structural factors: 1) the dynamics of the relationship between the diocesan hierarchy and the orders; and 2) the effect which the level of internal organization of the orders had on their "success".

The Orders and the Hierarchy

We have noted that some of the early monks were not only non-conformists, but in a very real sense, rebels. Even though Francis went out of his way to be loyal and had staunch friends in the hierarchy, his relationship to Rome, and the bishops generally, was tenuous. Clearly, the local clergy and bishops felt threatened by the orders. Partly this was due to the minimal control that could be exercised over them by the power-conscious diocesan structure. But it was also partly due to the popularity that the committed communities enjoyed among the common people. The movement was simply too popular to be frowned down.

It is probably no exaggeration to say that it took a thousand years for hierarchy and orders to learn to live together in the Roman Church. It may be that the dissolution of the Society of Jesus from 1773 until the early part of the nineteenth century was the climax of this educational process. Let's hope it doesn't take Protestantism so long.

As we've seen, Ireland did not have this particular problem locally. There the inverted jurisdiction, with the sodality in the lead position, did not seem to produce equivalent tensions. This should not surprise us. The more committed naturally threaten the average; not so the other way around.

Yet the Irish monastic structure found itself under constant pressure from the Roman hierarchy with its universal presuppositions and claims. And in this centuries-long struggle we have a classic case study in the relative strengths of structural models. As we've seen, the Irish structures had a very low profile and were rooted in their cultural soil. On the other hand, Roman Christianity was rooted less in a culture than in the organizational genius of a once-successful empire.

Structural Strength and Persistence

McNeill feels, apparently with considerable regret, that it was "inevitable" that the Roman system "would sooner or later absorb the relatively uncoordinated, dispersedly directed Celtic communities. With every encounter there would naturally come a loss of autonomy" (1974:193). The latter certainly happened at the Synod of Whitby as early as 664. But this ostensible Roman Catholic "victory" was certainly not assimilation. Even the lower level of administrative absorption was not complete at the turn of the millenium.

So while most historians focus on the "weakness" of the Irish structural forms, we might better ask the secret of their *strengths* which, seemingly without that much conscious effort, resisted for so long the initiative-impeding, machine-like efficiency of the Roman power structure. McNeill concedes that their lack of concern for widespread organization may have tended to limit somewhat the impact of their continental mission, great as it was. Yet there is no concealing his admiration for the route they chose. His brilliant retrospect deserves to be quoted at some length.

> Not less strange to us is the fact that nothing of all this was planned with consultation and forethought by master minds at any head office . . . It is an arresting fact, in [our] age of complicated organization and too little unity of spirit, that in the era of their free enterprise the Irish saints largely evangelized, and tutored in Latin culture, the Germanic world. Coming to pagan tribes almost as squatters in their midst and without ecclesiastical credentials, but in unquestioning obedience to "the heavenly vision" that filled their consciousness, they found a way of approach to the minds and spirits of their bearers. Without question, inherent vitality is what is essential to a church: organization is secondary and too easily becomes a hindrance to initiative (1974:224,225).

To which I can only add: Hear, hear!

For those who cannot identify with this Irish model and feel the need to run a tighter ship, I'd suggest a look at the Benedictine Rule. It is highly authoritarian but it is also flexible. It is human; it cares. This Rule was dominant in the monasticism of the West, and the Benedictine Order has persisted for nearly 15 centuries. We should add, however, that this kind of organizational persistence cannot be compared, one-for-one, with the six-century vitality of the Irish orders. Both had their ups and downs. But the deterioration/renewal cycles of the Roman orders seem much more pronounced.

In the Franciscan model, we see a structural combination of the Irish and the Benedictine, and the results are not encouraging. In some ways, Francis had the spirit of the Irish. He wanted simplicity in all things, including structure. His original Rule consisted of just a few precepts from the Gospels. When he returned from his famous encounter with the Muslim Sultan Malak-el-Kamel, "He found confusion and disunity, and it soon became apparent that the rule must be revised. A way of life that was possible for a small group of mendicant friars was proving inappropriate for an order with thousands of members" (Erikson 1970:44).

It is clear that Francis found this task very frustrating. He "repeatedly tried to reword the original form without forfeiting its pristine simplicity. The revised rules pleased no one, and dissention grew" (ibid). The task was eventually done, but presumably others had to take a hand. This was true also of the government of the order. Francis was clearly not an organizer or administrator. For this he leaned on one of his early companions, Brother Elias, who was more typically Roman. Even during Francis' relatively short life-time, parties were forming, and these turned into sharp divisions after his death. The Zealots or Spirituals held to Francis' original ideals. Others argued for a complete relaxation of the rule of poverty while the majority sought middle ground. In succeeding years the Franciscans have been rent by more schisms than any other large order. It would seem that the Benedictines and the Irish, with two quite opposite approaches, were both more successful in handling diversity and commitment.

As we look back on this pre-Reformation period of churchly development and Christian expansion, we've seen the re-birth of the sodality idea in a form initially quite inferior to the missionary

bands of the New Testament period. But the formation of these committed communities had a renewing effect on sections of the Church, and eventually provided more and more mobility for specific missionary expansion. These communities were often more tolerated than accepted by the diocesan structure, except in Ireland where the sodality structure was in the lead position.

Perhaps the biggest surprise we've uncovered is the attractiveness of the deeply committed community, particularly to the young. Yet a recent sociological study by a Christian churchman has drawn a similar conclusion: the higher the demand made by a religious group, the greater its appeal (Kelley 1971). In applying this principle to the Christian church, Kelley takes the usual mono-structural view — i.e. he views "the Church" only in terms of congregations and their linkages. However, his positive examples are mostly drawn from those church bodies that sociologists like to call sects. And as we'll see in the following chapter, sects, thus conceived, are committed communities that often *combine* many sodality characteristics with a more settled, nurturing role.

Those models are next on our tour. Here we return to Protestant country, roughly speaking. A pun is fully intended. For the treatment we'll see these committed "radical" groups receiving at the hands of the Reformers (on the one hand, and the Catholics on the other) was rough indeed!

CHAPTER 4

Radical Christians

A funny thing's happened to that word "radical" on the way to the twenty-first century. To illustrate this, I asked some of my former colleagues to play the word-association game. You know, the leader gives a trigger word, and the rest of the players write down the very first word or phrase they think of that they "associate" with it. The trigger word, in this case was "radical".

Nineteen adults of mixed ages "played". All but three of their responses are at least impliedly negative; 13 of these carry connotations that are rather clearly "bad". In fact, that very word was one such response — along with: trouble, extreme, revolt, revolutionist, Jerry Rubin and Jane Fonda! The 3 who wrote "student" were almost certainly not taking a positive view. The same could be said for: instigator, hippie, and hair!

By contrast, I checked out the definitions of radical in my two dictionaries. The one I bought as a college freshman (Webster's 1941) reads: "Proceeding from the root. Original; fundamental; reaching to the center or ultimate source; affecting the vital principle or principles." Well now, that's quite positive — particularly from a Christian perspective. Even the application to politics is very neutral: "Of or pertaining to radicals in politics."

In the 1966 edition we see the beginnings of change. Definition 2 reads, in part, "favoring fundamental or *extreme* change; specifically, favoring such change of the social structure; *very leftist*." The italics are mine.

Language, like culture, is always in a state of some change. Furthermore, language changes *reflect* cultural or social changes. And when society is in major change, as at present, currently significant words are apt to change more dramatically. That's clearly what has happened to "radical". This can tell us something important about what's happening to us. But I must hold that subject for Chapter 6.

Meanwhile, I need a word-tool. And the *original* meaning behind "radical" is exactly what I need. So that's the way I'm going to use the word — and the only way I'll use it, unless I qualify it at the time. In doing this, I'm not trying to turn back the clock, though I'll admit that I'd like to. The problem with "giving away" a word like this is finding a suitable replacement. Because of the lack of reasonable alternates, radical-as-root is worth rescuing. Still, I'd best leave that cause to others. I only ask you to accept my word-tool for the balance of this book.

As a first application of this tool, we can understand just what church historians are talking about when they speak of "Radical Christianity" in the period surrounding the Reformation. Popularly we lump together as Protestants all the non-Roman Western Christians who rose up against the corruption of the medieval Church. But more correctly we should distinguish between the Protestant Reformation and what is usually called the Radical Reformation. The former is the source of the mainline Protestant traditions: Lutheran, Reformed and Anglican (though many Anglicans do not think of themselves as Protestants). The latter is the genesis (some would say the *re*-birth or surfacing) of a number of smaller traditions collectively known as Anabaptists, Free Churches, Believers' Churches, or Radical Christianity.

How did the sodality concept fare amidst all the turmoil of those momentous years? To answer this, we'll have to follow the two streams separately, at least initially.

Protestant Blind Spots

First of all, the Protestant reformers rejected monasticism. This is not too surprising in view of their concern over the wealth, the power and the general corruption of many of the orders at that time. They also had a Germanic hostility to the Roman preoccupation with celibacy as the priestly model of sanctity. This issue seemed to them to be a cornerstone of the orders. Unfortunately, they made little or no attempt to reform or replace these sodality structures.

Latourette tends to defend this neglect by calling attention to the mammoth task the reformers faced in renewing the diocesan structure — to say nothing of just surviving the less-than-friendly attempts of the Roman Church to reabsorb them. Still he regrets this; for the lack of sodality "machinery" no doubt contributed significantly to the Protestants' 200-year delay in initiating missionary activities. At the same time, Luther had two additional reasons for by-passing the missionary task: he believed that the end of the world was so imminent that there wasn't time to spread the Gospel widely; he also held that the Great Commission had only been binding on the original Apostles (Latourette 1970b:25,26).

Nevertheless, Luther was quite aware, early on, of the levels-of-commitment factor we spoke of in chapter one. Noting how marginally many people involved themselves in worship at public services, he wrote in 1526 of the need for a "truly evangelical order" for those "who want to be Christians in *earnest* and who profess the gospel *with hand and mouth.*" They could "sign their names and meet alone in a house somewhere to pray, to read, to baptize, to receive the sacrament, and to *do other Christian works.*" He didn't feel he should organize the order himself lest it "turn into a sect." Rather, his strategy would be to concentrate on "public services for the people, until Christians who *earnestly* love the Word *find each other and join together*" (Luther 1965:63,64; all italics are mine).

Regrettably, Luther was unable to resolve a dilemma involved here. As Roland Bainton puts it,

> Luther wanted both a confessional church based on personal faith and experience, and a territorial church including all in a given locality. If he were forced to choose, he would take his stand with the masses, and this was the direction he moved (1950:311).

This included, of course, moving closer to the ruling princes for their help in securing the success of the Reformation. This further confirmed the national or territorial character of the new structures. So while the Protestant Reformation spoke to many important issues, church membership remained more closely linked to citizenship than commitment.

And this is part of what the Radical Reformation was all about. To the leaders of this movement, the reforms of Luther and Zwingli simply didn't go far enough; they viewed these as half-way measures. They called for a back-to-the-*roots*-of-our-faith approach, for which they are called "radical". Ironically, the alternative communities which they brought into being, suffered and died for, were in many ways the fulfillment of Luther's conceptualization of an evangelical order. "The tragedy of Protestantism is that when such groups did emerge in history, Luther and his colleagues could see nothing in them but enthusiasts, fanatics, and rebels. This prejudice has not been completely overcome to this day" (Durnbaugh 1968:4).

Radical Communities

Part of that "fanatical" image derives from the rejection, by most of these groups, of infant baptism. Even those groups that retained a strong covenantal outlook, emphasized conscious commitment through individual adult decisions. This, in its turn, led to convictions favoring adult-baptism — and the practice of re-baptizing, for which they were dubbed Anabaptists.

This stress on individual commitment was a universal hallmark of the movement. So, too, was its emphasis on selfless sharing which Littell calls a "community of consumption." The latter was quite thoroughgoing at times, but without much system and without compulsion. If we exclude the regrettable Münster community (the most notorious example of the truly fanatical fringe which gave the whole movement a bad name), only the Hutterian Brethren developed a total economic community; and even this was simply a more thorough and rigorously organized application of the widely held ideal of sharing (Littell 1958:96,97).

Consequently, the practice of community in its various forms and degrees must be understood in terms of the Anabaptist concept of discipleship. The latter was the basis of community, not the result. Twice in their history the Hutterites, for example, gave up their community of goods when their strong, vital faith waned. In such circumstances, the totality of community life became an unbearable burden. But with a revival of their faith and commitment came also a renewal of their unique community form (*ibid;* Horsch 1971:xvi).

During the last third of the sixteenth century, after two decades of forced dispersion to avoid annihilation, the Hutterites enjoyed a "golden age" of peace in which they founded at least one hundred *Brüderhofs* with a probable total membership of 30,000. The social accomplishments of these communities read more like the nineteenth or twentieth century than the sixteenth: efficiently managed industries, complete literacy (almost unheard of in that day) and advanced medical techniques that attracted even their adversaries. But more impressive even than their showplace model communities was the missionary concern of the Hutterites.

Missionary Energy

And in this missionary *concern,* the Hutterites by no means stood alone; this, too, was widespread among the radical groups. At the outset, this impulse was carried out primarily by journeying craftsmen and wandering lay preachers, some of whom were exiles or refugees from persecution. (We have noted this pattern in other areas.) But eventually persecution played a further role among these people; it seems to have "changed them from wandering pilgrims to missionary strategists, ready when the time came to be martyrs also." Littell sees this transition to a more intentional mission centering around two events. The first was the establishment of the Hutterite economy in Moravia. This provided a structure that put them in the forefront with the most extensive missionary activities. But a more specific event was the convening of the Martyr Synod of Augsburg in 1527, so named because only two or three of the participants lived to see the fifth year of the resultant missionary movement. As Littell says, it could as well have been called the Missionary Synod, for there the leaders of the movement "divided the land on a grand map of evangelical enterprise" (1958:120-122).

We must return now to an earlier question: given an identical period of history, why did the leaders of the two Reformation streams (Protestant and Radical) take such opposite views of missionary responsibility? Both were equally devoted to the Bible and drew their rationale from it. True to our thesis, we have seen one important difference in the stronger commitment of the Radical Christians. Historians have likened them to the "third order" of the Franciscans that we met in the last chapter. Continuing that figure, we might look on the "total" community of the Hutterites as a combination (that is, non-celibate) first/second order. And as noted, it was this strongest committed community of that era that accomplished the most in strategic, intentional missionary activity. So the mutually-supportive community structure again became the crucial means of deliberate outreach.

However, there was another force at work here, too. As we've already seen, Luther once had the necessary insight by which such committed communities might have been developed *within* the Protestant Reformation. But his decision to link forces with the prince committed all his energy and resources toward a church for all citizens where the least common denominator was very least indeed. As if this overly-inclusivist character of the "territorial church" was not a large enough problem, the situation got worse. "The bloody battles of the religious wars (in which, it may be admitted, religion was sometimes the pretext for other aims by the rulers) were only stopped by the compromise of territorialism. 'As the prince, so the religion' was the solution . . . [of] the Peace of Westphalia" (Durnbaugh 1968:228). With this carving up of the map of Europe, one can easily see why George Williams (1962) often uses the term Magisterial Reformation for what we have been calling the Protestant Reformation. The implication for missionary activity was to make it more difficult for each church to break out of its boundary — at least until the Protestant nations began to wrest control of the seas from Catholic Spain.

As we've already noted, the Radical Christians had met earlier to carve up the same map. But the missionary implications of this act were just the opposite. And since they were unencumbered with princely allegiance, they were free to act upon their direct interpretation of the New Testament missionary mandate. And act they did.

I suspect that most of my readers while making their way through the last several pages will have experienced a certain uneasiness about the credibility of the material. If you haven't yet formulated your questions, let me see if I can help. In the first place, if these Radical Churches of the Reformation period were so vital and so missionary, why are they so little known (compared to the Protestant Reformation)? Furthermore, how does this picture of aggressive, out-reaching communities back there square with the present image of some of their successors (certain Mennonite and

Hutterite groups) as *enclosed* communities? These are fair questions. And the answers have a direct bearing on our task of trying to draw lessons from historical models.

One obvious answer to the first question relates to relative size. The very "magisterial" or territorially inclusivist nature of the Protestant stream gave it wider scope. By rejecting official status and stressing individual commitment, the Radical Churches had to start smaller. Their power to attract was at least as strong as the earlier committed communities we've been examining. But the tendency we've also noted for such communities to threaten the diocesan structure was even stronger. After all, this movement didn't start with a few hermits making off to the desert; here were whole families posing a directly competitive threat. Furthermore, they posed this felt-threat to not one but *two* establishments: the Roman (or, in some cases, the Eastern) Church, and the emerging Protestants. The resultant two-pronged persecution became exceedingly physical at times, and the brutal means employed understandably frightened away all but the most committed and courageous. Even the latter were kept yet smaller in number, and relatively leaderless, by the abundance of largely Protestant-inspired executions.

Then, too, it is a fact of history that persecuted minorities experience suppression not only of their ideas and their numbers, but also of their memory. Until relatively modern times, only victorious regimes or establishments wrote the history books. Minority accomplishments were, at best, ignored; if their protest was sufficiently threatening to the vested interests, records were often destroyed as ruthlessly as the people! Consequently, it takes a lot of patient research, and often some happy accidents, to piece together the ignored, and sometimes suppressed, histories of prophetic minorities. In the past two decades, a resurgent interest in the Radical Reformation has stimulated such research, resulting in a number of important books to which I am greatly indebted for the development of this chapter. The same is true of Irish Christianity as discussed in the previous chapter. We owe much appreciation to these researchers, for very often the best re-usable models emerge from the records of suppressed movements. This is particularly true of our present study.

While suppressive persecution can explain the visibly limited long-range success of the Radical Reformation, we have yet to deal with the question of how it became enclosed. Littell, one of the abler modern apologists of the movement, readily admits that "today, the most direct descendants of militant Anabaptism reside in cultural enclaves in America . . . [where they] represent an archaic social pattern strangely out of place in the twentieth century. Plain clothes have become peculiar clothes" (1958:75). All radical movements, in reaching back to their roots, have a tendency to exalt the primitive. Within Christianity, such radicalism or primitivism reaches back spiritually to the New Testament. But something else can also happen. As Littell puts it, "a structure of religious primitivism tends to slip over into a pattern of cultural primitivism" *(ibid.)*. And surely this tendency was later reinforced in the Radical Christians by a growing weariness with the prophetic role. In the light of repeated rejection and persecution, we can sympathize with their eventual withdrawal from the tensions involved in confronting a hostile world, choosing rather to live out their principles internally. But their forgivable drift to cultural primitivism should alert us to this inherent risk involved in all radical movements. We'll have more to say about this when we deal with current communitarian movements in a later chapter.

Pietism: Committed Protestants

Now we must move along to the latter part of the seventeenth century when a renewal movement *within* mainstream Protestantism took on those characteristics of an "evangelical order" which Luther first espoused and later fought. I'm referring to what we call Pietism. And once more we are faced with a problem of "image" in twentieth century America. The very name of the movement sounds too "holy Joe" for us; we tend to associate piety with pretence rather than with righteousness. And those who are generally acquainted with the original movement tend to equate it with a one-sided soul-saving emphasis. Such, until recently, was the stereotype I held also.

That's not, however, the way the Pietists saw themselves. On the contrary, they tended to express their religious idealism with such words as "whole", "perfect" or "entire". They contended that the movement was simply a second phase of the Reformation — an extension of the reform principle to the Christian life, whereas the original Protestant reformers had concentrated mainly on doctrine and polity (Stoeffler 1965:16,23). Like every reform movement in history, Pietism encountered the risk of the pendulum swing and met the challenge with something short of perfection.

Nevertheless, Pietism was a potent renewing force within Protestantism, and self-consciously so. While the emphasis on a deeper individual commitment again proved threatening to the church at large, opposition generally took more tolerable forms than that experienced by the Radical Christians. Equally in contrast to the earlier movement were: a stronger determination to remain within the established Church, and an avoidance of doctrinal novelty. Despite this, some groups were eventually squeezed out; but this was normally a gradual rather than an eruptive process.

To meet the special needs of its adherents in this situation, Pietism developed a structure sometimes called the conventicle.

> To the Pietist's way of thinking the territorial church to which belonged everybody who had been born and baptized in a given geographical locality could not possibly meet the religious needs of the more earnest Christians. Its theology, psychology, and ethic, its worship, preaching, and instruction were felt to be geared to the religious level of the masses. Hence some means had to be found to provide for meeting the religious needs of those men and women who wanted something more than baptism, confirmation, and a learned sermon on some disputed point of theology. The result was . . . the conventicle on Sunday afternoon in which the sermon was further discussed, in which laymen testified to its truth, and in which its implications for daily life became focal points for mutual exhortation (ibid:19,20).

Philip Jacob Spener, usually regarded as the founder of the movement, referred to these cell groups as *ecclesiolae in ecclesia*, the little churches in the Church. This concept of a committed growth group, which is enjoying a significant revival today, gave some form to the movement.

Very early, the movement on the Continent also acquired a center. August Francke, a younger contemporary of Spener, became the most dominant figure on the theological faculty at the University of Halle. Here he founded schools in which he introduced innovative programs bathed in the atmosphere of

Pietism (Latourette 1953:896). It was from this center that Protestantism, at long last, embarked purposefully on the cross-cultural missionary task.

Two of Francke's young proteges, Bartholomew Ziegenbalg and Henry Plütschau, sailed for India in 1705. The problems these pioneers faced were phenomenal. And the statistical results of their mission were modest. Nevertheless, they blazed a trail and developed some methodological criteria for those who would follow (Neill 1964:228-231). Beyond that, their lives and their work influenced an impressionable young Count who enrolled in 1710 at Halle. Besides being exposed to regular reports of the pioneer venture, Count Ludwig von Zinzendorf met Plütschau when he visited Halle in 1713; in 1715 Ziegenbalg came from India to Halle where he married the sister of one of the Count's friends (Danker 1971:18).

The Two Streams Merge: The Moravians

It is through this Count Zinzendorf that the Protestant-Pietist stream merges with some descendants of Radical Christianity to form the most significant missionary movement of the eighteenth century. And since this mission of the Moravians was carried out in the context of a near-total community, we should take a little closer look at this model.

The ancient *Unitas Fratrum,* or Unity of the Brethren, actually pre-dates Luther's theses-posting incident, as well as the main body of the Radical Reformation, by half a century. But these Czech Christians, spiritual descendents of John Hus, were an early part of the radical stream. They experienced similar recurrent cycles of persecution and relative peace until the 1620's when the movement was scattered and driven underground. A century later, a small group encouraged by a traveling carpenter crossed the nearby German border to seek refuge on Count Zinzendorf's estate at a place called Herrnhut.

What began as a refugee settlement was soon transformed by a profound spiritual awakening into a strong committed community, complete with written statutes resembling the *Disciplinae* of their predecessors and the *Regula* of the still earlier orders. Latourette's perceptive analysis of the Moravians has been widely quoted, and with good reason. It is worth repeating here.

Here was a new phenomenon in the expansion of Christianity, an entire community, of families as well as of the unmarried, devoted to the propagation of the faith. In its singleness of aim it resembled some of the monastic orders of earlier centuries, but these were made up of celibates. Here was a fellowship of Christians, of laity and clergy, of men and women, marrying and rearing families, with much of the quietism of the monastery and of Pietism but with the spread of the Christian message as a major objective, not of a minority of the membership, but of the group as a whole (1970b:47).

I would agree that the involvement of this whole community in the missionary task appears to be a new phenomenon. Yet the internal structure of the Moravian community is quite reminiscent of the Hutterite *Brüderhofs* we've already encountered, and they, too, formed the base of a strong missionary outreach. Perhaps the more extensive success of the Moravians is a reflection of what the earlier Hutterites might have accomplished had they lived in quieter times. This difference of environments may also be part of the reason why the Moravian communities avoided becoming enclosed.

They did not avoid, however, becoming a "church" — that is, a predominantly nurturing structure for a membership with varying levels of commitment. This is inevitable where families are involved. Even though adult decisions are stressed, it is difficult to maintain the sodality character and commitment of the founding group over many generations. On the one hand, this inevitability validates the rationale of celibate orders. But another approach is to raise the question we discussed at the end of the previous chapter: is the long-range persistence of a particular sodality structure that vital? And the Moravian model provides a good platform for examining this further.

In the first place, we should not put the whole stress on *non*-persistence. The fact is that the Moravians continued to be a very vital missionary community for well over a century. These committed people *were* successful in passing their vision along for quite a few generations.

A second factor worth noting is how well this movement served its particular historical time slot. As we've seen, Pietism awakened Protestant missionary vision, including the lands far beyond the borders of Europe. This produced isolated pioneer efforts like those of Ziegenbalg and Plütschau. A few scattered missionary societies also appeared. But the time was not yet ripe for the full development of the society approach: this was to belong to the nineteenth century. Meanwhile, the migrating Moravian missionaries, forming mutually-supportive, largely self-sustaining communities, fitted nicely into the eighteenth century environment.

Finally, the Moravians, like many vital movements before and since, have had some of their most extensive fruitage in other movements which they strongly influenced. The most visible example is the Methodist movement which derived some of its spiritual power from the acknowledged influence of the Moravians on John Wesley both during his early years in Georgia and on a later visit to Herrnhut. Wesley also partly patterned his famed small-group "classes" on the *Banden* of the Moravians which were voluntary fellowship communities within the larger total community.

If a committed community can keep its sodality character alive long enough to carry out its mission in its time, and particularly if it can reproduce itself in new successor movements, becoming a broader nurturing structure may just possibly be its best destiny. This probably is preferable to enclosure. And it is certainly better than keeping alive a form that has, for the present, ceased to have any really relevant function in a changing world. What we're brushing against here, of course, is the age-old problem of new wine and old wine skins. And we'll have to return to it again.

Now just before summing up and turning to the explosive burst of missionary energy released in the nineteenth century, we should comment just a bit further on the self-supporting nature of the Moravian missions. William Danker (1971) has devoted half a book to this financial support model, pointing out that the cultural bias of American Christians (which we will see developing in the next chapter) has hindered our objective consideration of this option. Danker is primarily concerned that American missionaries not infect the churches they plant with our "collection plate economy" bias. But we must also consider the radically-changing American economy of the mid-1970's which may well *force* us to consider alternative missionary support structures for our own continuing efforts.

To be sure, we can hardly swallow the Moravian model whole.

Their communities were built primarily around crafts, and became progressively less valid as the Industrial Revolution progressed. But there are principles here that we can *apply*. And while avoiding any sentimental primitivism, we might even find a certain kinship with the Moravian craftsmen in a day when validly radical Christianity must join its secular counterparts in challenging the growing dominance and destructive potential of technology.

Looking back, we see that Protestantism (now broadly defined) did not get off to a very good start in learning to live with the sodality concept. The blood of martyrs was even more dramatically the seed of *this* structure of the Church. The committed communities existed from the beginning and persisted; but for most of this period they lived primarily in separation from the territorial churches, sometimes by choice but more often of necessity.

Non-celibate communitarian life styles were developed on a wide variety of levels. The correlation of community structure and missionary involvement was notable. (On the other hand, nationalism or territorialism tended to work against missionary outreach.) Yet the higher potential of the more structured community involved an attendant risk of sliding into cultural enclosure. The opposite potential is transition from sodality character to a predominantly nurturing structure. This is not necessarily an undesirable result.

Because the committed community structures were forced to exist in separation from the Protestant mainstream, the latter neglected the missionary mandate for two centuries. The sodality-like radical churches, however, acted on their missionary zeal even though limited by the turbulence of the period. In the eighteenth century, when Protestants finally got involved in missions on a world basis, it was the Moravian community, combining the strongest elements of both Reformation streams, that played the pace-setting role.

What they set the pace *for* is just ahead: the amazing burst of voluntary action that, in terms of *missionary* models, is the truly grand finale of our tour. Mission historian Kenneth Latourette had good reason for calling the nineteenth "The Great Century."

This is truly familiar territory. But here, too, we must not get too caught up with the scenic, popular view. There may well be some un-posted dead end roads.

CHAPTER 5

Voluntary Societies

Just 200 years ago (as I write this) some unknown person at Lexington, Massachusetts, fired a "shot heard around the world." I presume there are many people around today's world, weary of America's dominance, who would consider this historical slogan as just one more yankee pretension. I don't blame them. But in this case the slogan just happens to be true.

The initial shock waves, reverberating first through the western world, carried the message: ordinary people do count, after all; they do have personal worth and they can realize worthwhile accomplishments in groupings of their own choice — without the leave or aid of the aristocracy. As a result of such feelings, the voluntary society became a significant sociological phenomenon of the nineteenth century. And it was through this form of association that Protestant Christians belatedly went forth *in numbers* to share their faith with the whole world.

Revival and Response

To be sure, this new wave of missionary activity had other roots besides the American Revolution. Of these, the most crucial was the eighteenth century spiritual movement known in Britain as The Evangelical Awakening, and in America as The Great Awakening. This movement had a world-wide character, affecting also Protestants in continental Europe and elsewhere, but the impact on the English-speaking Atlantic community was particularly decisive.

For here it raised the commitment level of a significant percentage of Protestants and gave these renewed Christians a sense of unity across confessional lines. Usually referred to as Evangelicalism, this ecumenical atmosphere arising out of the Awakenings was a movement quite without structural form; though it was to find a variety of active expressions through the voluntary societies we've mentioned and will be examining further.

This brief background sketch identifies the source of commitment and the structural form on which the new missionary wave was built. And we're conscious of some new elements here. First, the heightened commitment of God's people was a more positive factor. Oh, there was plenty to react against in the eighteenth century, too. But this involved moral bankruptcy in society rather than deterioration within the Church. In fact, church leadership was also affected by the wide-spread renewal, so some of the tensions we've noted in previous chapters were less apparent, at least initially. And as soon as the structural forms developed, the movement rather quickly turned outward in service, further postponing the inevitable tensions.

We should note in passing that these renewed Christians did not express their commitment in evangelistic missions alone. They also became very much involved in combating the social ills of their day: prison reform, the treatment of the mentally ill, factory reform — particularly in England where the unhappy by-products of the Industrial Revolution developed so early — and, most importantly, the growing abolition movement. In these areas of service also, the voluntary society became the structural form of channeling their commitment.

In one sense the voluntary society was not new. All the committed communities we've been examining were voluntary associations as far as membership was concerned. But in most of those historical communities, commitment was first expressed in terms of life style (including commitment to the community) only later in terms of task or cause. Now the task itself became the initiating focal point of these new societies. Whatever community spirit developed was a result, not the foundational factor it had been in the earlier models.

If something was lost here, it was not lost entirely; and something else was gained that was crucial to the historical period involved.

Doors were opening to evangelistic witness all over the world and "opportunity" seemed to be written in large letters over the door-posts. The involvement of large numbers was needed. The Awakenings (including several follow-up awakenings: at the end of the eighteenth century, in the 1830's and again just before the American Civil War) provided a larger percentage of committed Christians; the new-style task-oriented societies provided the vehicle for enlisting them in large numbers.

Here/There Commitment

And that enlistment did not involve only the steadily growing number of the highly committed who boarded ships to cross the ocean. The committed Christians who remained at home and supported them felt very deeply involved. In some of the missionary sending societies, these supporting Christians were just as much members as those who sailed away — the committed-here supporting the committed-there. This particular sodality form for expressing the unity of the committed members, here and there, persists to this day in the Church Missionary Society (Anglican).

William Carey is widely acknowledged as the founder of the modern Protestant missionary movement, and his 1792 essay with the long, long title is acknowledged as the founding document: *An Enquiry into the Obligations of Christians to Use Means for the Conversion of the Heathens*. By his term "means", Carey was referring, in part, to the voluntary society idea which was then still in its infancy. Toward the end of his essay he proposes:

> Suppose a company of serious Christians, ministers and private persons, were to form themselves into a society, and make a number of rules respecting the regulation of the plan, and the persons who are to be employed as missionaries, the means of defraying the expence, etc. etc. This society must consist of persons whose hearts are in the work, men of serious religion, and possessing a spirit of perseverance; there must be a determination not to admit any person who is not of this description, or to retain him longer than he answers to it (Carey 1961:82,83).

In the second of those two long sentences, Carey is clearly referring to all the members, here and there, and not just to "the persons who are to be employed as missionaries." Note that above-average commitment was expected of *all* these members; and all were subject to what Kelley calls "the power of the gate" (1972:125).

Again, we've seen similar patterns before. The Irish *paruchia* had such a here/there community link. The Franciscan missionaries had ties not only with the brothers and sisters of their communities, but with the members of their third order as well. The Moravian synthesis, through which couples and families were included in more distant missionary efforts, was probably the strongest form of here/there community in the modern period. While the voluntary societies which began proliferating 60 years later lacked this depth, they succeeded, as we've noted, in involving many more people.

The involvement of the larger "here" community was achieved through the medium of money. I suspect that most American Christians would react to that statement the way I once would have: so what else isn't new? Yet that is just the surprising point; it *was* relatively new. In fact, the very term, voluntarism, was introduced to contrast their voluntary contributions with the church tax approach of the European state churches. As we have noted, those earlier non-territorial churches that were most successfully missionary, the Hutterites, and later the Moravians, were largely self-supporting via their strong communal life style. Before that, the Catholic orders depended heavily on the patronage (often in the form of land endowments) or royalty and the nobility to carry out their missions. Even the pioneer missionaries of Pietism, Ziegenbalg and Plütschau, first went to India under the patronage of the Danish king. Only gifts from the third order of the Franciscans reflected a significant precedent for what was now developing. Coins in the begging bowls of the mendicant friars hardly involved the same kind of community motivation.

Involvement has again become a key word in the 1960's and 70's. But today's involvement-oriented Christian usually wants a piece of the action beyond "merely" putting money in a collection plate. Consequently, it's hard for us to identify with our brethren of early nineteenth century America. Caught up in the spiritual renewal plus the we-can-do-it euphoria, they considered it a thrilling privilege to participate via the same offering-bringing act that has become so routine and impersonal to many people today. The form is the same; but the functional effect is quite different.

This contrasting functional effect should tell us something very important. For in looking at the rise of the voluntary societies we are not just looking at a model "back there." No, we're looking at the genesis of the principal form of missionary sodality throughout Protestantism today. Perhaps the collection-plate support feature is not the only sub-form of this movement whose function has fallen on hard times.

Indeed, a principle objective of this chapter is to consider various elements of this current sodality form in terms of continuing relevance or impairment. At the same time, we want to continue to note how this structure served from 1800 *to* the present. As in the case of the still-earlier models "back there", some vital element might have dropped out enroute which can be re-applied with telling effect today.

Societies as Communities

We find one such element as we probe these new societies for that commitment-to-each-other type of community we've been tracing through history. So far we've pictured the community aspect of these voluntary societies like a river in flood-tide: covering more of the landscape, yet not as deep for most of its width. But we don't want to go to the other extreme and think of it as "shallow". After all, shallow movements do not persist for nearly two centuries! Where we do find this strong sense of committed brotherhood is in some of the "there" components of these communities — that is, among the overseas missionaries. Consider, for example, the five young men who sailed for India in 1812 as the first missionaries of the newly-formed American Board of Commissioners for Foreign Missions (ABCFM). These men already had a strong bond between them as members of a student prayer group that had its roots in the famous haystack prayer meeting. They signed the petition that brought this interdenominational "American Board" to birth. And they sailed simultaneously for India, along with their young brides who shared their deep commitment.

At mid-century we find Rufus Anderson, senior secretary of the ABCFM and towering missionary strategist of his time, including in one of his annual reports the crucial need for such community within each mission of the Board (that is, the Board's missionary staff in each foreign country).

As soon as a mission contains three or more missionaries, it is expected to organize itself as a self-governing community . . . Mutual watchfulness thus becomes the official duty of each member. It is also in a high sense the interest of each one to exercise a fraternal watchfulness over his brethren (Beaver 1967:135).

How well this community concept fared in Anderson's time and the following decades is a matter of conjecture. But we do know that by the middle of the *twentieth* century a good many missionaries frankly admitted that their number one problem was their fellow missionaries. Certainly notable exceptions exist. But by and large we seem to have missed Anderson's target by a considerable margin. Today we normally deal with the resultant inter-personal problems in two ways. We look at them as spiritual problems and through spiritual counsel encourage the missionaries toward personal growth and reconciliation. We also utilize professional counseling by qualified Christian psychologists. I heartily endorse both of these remedial approaches. But they are only remedial; they do not get at the root of the matter: the gradual loss of community.

We've noted that the first foreign missionaries of the ABCFM applied and were appointed as a group. The men involved had an already-developed sense of community from their student days. This may have been duplicated occasionally in later appointments, but inevitably most applicants to this kind of society would be selected on an individual basis. Initially, this probably did not work against the building of communal spirit overseas as per Anderson's model. For though the ABCFM was, on paper, national and interdenominational, it was then very much a New England affair involving churches that were similar confessionally and further bound together by the Evangelicalism mentioned above. The candidates were drawn from a relatively small Christian population in a fairly compact area and had a great deal in common.

As the country grew, and as this and other national societies extended their constituencies, this commonality was gradually diluted. Later in the century, waves of immigration introduced further diversity which eventually showed up in Protestant societies in the present century. This evolved heterogeneity was a long way from the fraternity of that 1812 pioneer band; and even farther from the ethnic, confessional and communal cohesion of the Moravian missions. Furthermore, Western society in general, and American society in particular, was increasingly individualistic. This is not very fertile soil for growing strong communities.

When I became involved with a new mission society in the mid-1940's, I was much impressed with a very readable little book written for missionary candidates by two experienced missionaries to the orient. Entitled *Ambassadors for Christ* (Cable 1946), it discusses the practical aspects of missionary life with a candor that was not all that common in 1935 when it was first published. More specifically, it is a handbook on how to cope with the problems posed by the particular kind of evolved sodalities we've been examining. One highly revealing passage illustrates what was happening to inter-personal dynamics; a single missionary on her first furlough shares with several trusted friends her experience under a "senior missionary",

> "There seemed to be no point of contact between us, though honestly I tried every way to find one . . . Strangely enough, though we had both signed the same basis of belief, our points of view were totally different and we had no fellowship in the things of the spirit . . . I was sensitive about having been forced into what, after all, was her home, by people who never took the time or trouble to realise the obvious incompatibility of our temperaments. Those five years were a wretched time, during which I fought steadily against a domination to which, though I bowed my head, I never dared to yield in spirit . . . After five years I was moved, and then things were different, but that first experience has stamped me for life."

> There was silence in the group as each woman present made her offering of unspoken sympathy to the once vivacious Betty, now so sobered and self-contained *(ibid:*118,119).

Mission Management

These perceptive authors have not only highlighted a condition, but have accurately fingered one of the causes: how these mission societies are administered. We must now trace the evolution of this leadership even though it is personally threatening to me. For I participated in such administration for 27 years and have many close friends (until now!) who are still so engaged.

For a starting point, let's go back to Rufus Anderson and that 1848 report we've already quoted from. In this, he brings out the necessary, foundational corollaries for the kind of self-governing overseas community he advocated: careful selection of personnel and thoughtful restraint on the part of the Board in carrying out its oversight function.

> Missionaries should be employed who *deserve* confidence, and then confidence should be reposed in them; nor should results be required, which are beyond the power of their labors to produce. Many things which, at first, it might seem desirable for the Board to do, are found, on a nearer view, to lie entirely beyond its jurisdiction; so that to attempt them would be useless, nay, a ruinous usurpation (Beaver 1967:130).

The quality of partnership and level of trust reflected in that statement has certainly not disappeared from mission administration today. But it has been significantly impaired. The reasons are sociological and even technological. As Bishop Neill puts it, "The invention of the electric telegraph spoiled all." In Carey's day an exchange of letters took about a year. Of necessity, decision-making resided principally with the missionary and the field community. "As communications improved and became more speedy, at every turn the missionary had to refer matters to his home board or committee" (Neill 1964:510). This centralizing trend has steadily worked against community.

Technology has had a further effect on mission administration which has only become fully visible in the past decade or two. I'm speaking now about the development of management science. Throughout the period we've been discussing, the Industrial Revolution steadily changed the character of American business from small, local, village (or, at least, neighborhood) enterprises, to ever-larger production facilities which hired individuals from a wide variety of backgrounds. Exploitation of workers in the early industrial period was gradually relieved under pressure from the unions, public opinion and, in due course, legislation. Eventually industry teamed with the behavioral sciences in a more "enlightened" approach. I use quotes because many people today question the motivation of management science. It's concern for the individual and his sense of fulfillment is, they say, basically manipulative and differs from the earlier exploitation only in its subtility. Bob Townsend of Avis rent-a-car fame ("We're only No. 2.") virtually admits this in his best-selling *Up the Organization* (1970:142), while at the same time he clearly does, in his own way, care about his people. We need not debate here the relative humanitarianism of this admittedly profit-motivated science, though in our applications of it we should never lose sight of its deepest materialistic tap root.

More directly applicable to *mission* administration is the pragmatic acceptance by management science of individualism and heterogeneity. These are the sociological givens of industrial management. It's one thing to recognize the realistic existence of these factors, as we have done earlier. But to accept them as inevitable is something else. For then these become the building blocks of personnel management, and foreclose the search for community in opposition to these forces.

There are at least two reasons, I feel, why mission administrations edged toward this philosophical trend of the business model. The first ties in with the centralizing trend we've noted. Control gravitated toward the home boards, which now included Christian business men as well as ministers. To many of these men the mission movement seemed to be sloppily managed. Sometimes this was regrettably true, by any standard of measurement. So the influence of these laymen became one stimulus for mission administrators to sit at the feet of management science.

The Sodality as Church

Quite apart from this, the voluntary societies eventually faced the same struggle for identity and existence within the Church that we have noted in earlier sodality models. The strong ecumenical spirit of Evangelicalism, rooted in the Awakenings, faced steady dilution as the nineteenth century progressed. In America, one denomination after another withdrew from the cooperative missionary societies (like the "American Board") in order to form its own denominational mission board. This loss of united effort was sad enough; but what lay behind it was even sadder, though not unexpected in the light of history: outright ecclesiastical hostility to the sodality concept.

A classical case for church boards as opposed to voluntary societies was spelled out by the Protestant Episcopal Bishop Hobart in 1818, who emphasized that the Church, after all, was a "sacred institution . . . founded by a divine hand . . . and governed by him, [while the voluntary] associations . . . have no higher origin than human power and no object but human policy" (Winter 1970:38).

As we'll see shortly, voluntarism in Britain produced some sodality apologists who ably countered such one-sided ecclesiology. But until recently their writings were not well known in America where mission leadership has consciously or unconsciously struggled with questions of identity. Some of us too readily settled for categorizations of our structures like "extra-biblical" and "necessary expedients." I can recall discussions with my colleagues about the "part-church, part-business" nature of our structures, particularly in regard to the question of management and control. It was this kind of thinking that nudged me into the books and classrooms of management science.

Most (but not all) American mission societies today, denominational and otherwise, are structured on the business management model. Some may fall far short of achieving its desired efficiency, but this does not mean that they are exceptions. Others have more successfully applied the best management principles, moved much decision-making back to the field and become more people-sensitive. Given an adequate dosage of this sensitivity, some renewed sense of community might occasionally happen. But this is not built into the model.

You will note that we're not talking only about insights or applications drawn from business management. We're talking about certain foundational philosophies — both theirs and ours — of which we are hardly even conscious. Personally I feel that we must start afresh with a clear and firm premise: the mission sodality is not a business, it is one expression of the Church.

Where missionaries are, there is the Church; and there missionaries are responsible to demonstrate the reality of Christian community. The real point of tension therefore is between the Church as the community of God's people and *institutional expressions* of the Church (Snyder 1975:167; italics are mine).

Snyder's point is that *both* nurturing structures *and* sodalities are "institutional expressions" of the Church.

Building on this premise, insights can be drawn from a wide variety of sources of which the business world is only one. And freed from the basic management model, we can leave behind coordination of skilled individuals and aim straight for enablement of communities of gifted persons.

Such communities must emerge, yea, be planned for, if the evolved voluntary societies we have inherited are to continue as effective sodalities in our time. Why? In the following chapters I will attempt to show why many of tomorrow's (and even today's) missionary candidates will not find validity in anything less. But there's a more immediate reason. Our present missionary staffs need community because it is the only real solution to their largest unmet need: pastoral care.

Who is the missionary's pastor? This question has received a lot of discussion lately, and various schools have come up with a variety of answers. Management advocates sometimes talk as though the immediate supervisor in a mission situation can perform this role. It probably can happen. But again, it is certainly not built into the structure. In fact, a by-product of the business management model is to bring these two roles into conflict. Then there are the idealists who say that if we could only conquer our racism, the national pastor can minister to the foreign missionary. This not only can but does happen — in isolated cases. The real problem involved here is not racial but cultural. It can be just as acute between a Presbyterian pastor and a Jesus person in Southern California. When we hurt, we need a listener who not only loves us but also understands us.

More recently a school of thought which I appreciate and, by and large, identify with, has produced some strong advocates for pastoral care of the missionary by his home church and its pastor. (We might call this the body-life school, after Stedman's 1970 book title.) Considering the distance involved, the length of missionary terms, and pastoral changes, this seems quite unrealistic; but it has probably achieved some additional credence due to the paucity of other solutions. Not that its chief advocates see it as an expedient; to them it is rooted deeply in their ecclesiology with its congregational emphasis. We might even call it a community emphasis. But insofar as this ecclesiology is mono-structural, it sees the community only in terms of itself and can quite miss the ought-to-be-obvious potential of a second-decision community in far-off India with a body life of its own.

If the body-life churchmen could find room in their ecclesiology for the sodality — not just as mission vehicle, but as another valid expression of the Body, the Church — and if mission leadership could effectively trade in its hand-me-down business management chassis for a current, committed community model, we might find ourselves with some newly attractive and effective sodalities. Not that they would achieve easy and universal acceptance. For the ecclesiastical hostility we've noted is not only still alive but sometimes potently destructive — particularly within the mainline denominations. Some of the latter's original mission structures have been so submerged by reorganization that they are virtually obliterated. This, too, has been done in the name of management efficiency — and a fuzzied re-definition of "mission". In these larger hierarchical circles we have a particularly long way to go to achieve co-habitation of the two structures.

The Two Structures in Tension

For encouragement that this is attainable, however, we turn to the most hierarchical of all Protestant traditions: the Church of England. Here we find a small vanguard of voluntarism that even predates the Moravians. For example, The Society for the Propagation of the Gospel in Foreign Parts was founded in 1701 for the support of clergy to minister to "the King's loving subjects" in British colonies. However, its charter also purposed "the winning to the Christian faith of the aborigines and the Negro slaves in these possessions" (Latourette 1970b:49).

But the stronger Anglican model for our purposes is the Church Missionary Society, or CMS, to which we've already referred as an example of here/there community involvement. This society, founded in 1799 as the new burst of voluntarism began to blossom, has not only survived but thrived for 175 years as a true Protestant missionary "order" with a clear-cut life of its own while still in vital relationship to the diocesan structure. That relationship was not maintained without a struggle. Anglicans, too, were novices at this matter of living with sodalities. But in this particular struggle they have probably gained more ground than any other Protestants. We do well to learn from them.

One doesn't have to look far to find the reason for this progress. The CMS has enjoyed strong, reflective leadership, and several of these men worked diligently to establish the validity of the voluntary society. Henry Venn was a contemporary of Rufus Anderson and an equally brilliant missionary strategist. Some of his writings have been compiled and edited by a later occupant of his office, Max Warren. Here we find extracts on subjects like "The Voluntary Principle" and "The Independence of a Voluntary Society." Warren also includes part of a letter Venn wrote to the Archbishop of York "re proposal to establish a Central Board of Missions." Respectfully but firmly Venn tells the Archbishop that "A controlling Board of Missions would be an interference with the fundamental principles of the Society" the constitution of which, he reminds him, "has been from its very cradle that of a *voluntary society.*" The emphasis is Venn's! (Warren 1971:131-134).

It would appear that Venn played a significant role in resisting the centralizing trend in the Anglican communion. Because of the nature of episcopacy this had to include very careful definition of the delicate relationship between CMS missionaries and the bishops (*ibid:*143-173). As one who has lived quite outside of episcopacy, I find it remarkable that both Catholics and Anglicans have found their way through to the kind of relationship between the sodality and the ecclesiastical hierarchy that has largely escaped the rest of us. It is true, of course, that the Anglican tradition embraces a wide spectrum of outlook. But it would appear that much credit must go to the sodality leadership, not only for articulating their position capably, but also for their painstaking loyalty to their Anglican tradition.

Max Warren's interest in the voluntary principle went far beyond editing Venn's writings. He wrote repeatedly on this theme himself. He was the chief spokesman for those who strongly resisted the integration of the International Missionary Council into the WCC. In his recently-published autobiography, Warren summarizes the grounds of his opposition to that merger, "because I believe a vital issue of far-reaching importance is involved — something far deeper in its spiritual significance than an administrative marriage" (1974:157). In this summary he deals tellingly with the oft-repeated pronouncement of the ecclesiastically-minded WCC leadership that the entire church is a mission society. And he does this by calling attention to the importance — for the *whole* church — of a committed elite or vanguard. Warren does not deny that the whole Church and each of its members is

. . . called to Mission. But to be called and to be committed are two sadly different things. A community becomes committed precisely in proportion as it has a spiritual vanguard which is *committed*. It does not help towards strengthening this vanguard to pretend that every member of the Church is already part of it. Indeed my own conviction is that to have a unified missionary organisation actually obscures the real situation and prevents the average person ever making any progress at all towards becoming one of the vanguard. This is best achieved by voluntary organisations consisting of persons who have joined together on some agreed basis to pursue an agreed aim by agreed methods. If one believes this with all one's heart one is of necessity opposed to the creation of monolithic structures *(ibid:*158).

Warren believes that the IMC-WCC merger was based on a misconception of the distinctive roles of what he calls "organs of co-ordination and organs of voluntary action." He sees this principle operative not only in the Church, but in society generally. He recognizes that it produces tension, but maintains that "if a society is to be genuinely dynamic then it must accept the inevitability of tension."

Organs of co-ordination are necessary. Without them no community can exist beyond the smallest unit. But those who serve on these organs of co-ordination must be, in general, people whose 'bent' and 'spirit' drives them in the direction of co-ordination. It is an outlook on life which is a valid one and quite indispensable if the complexity of our world is to be brought under any effective control at all — if, theologically speaking, it is to be 'baptised into Christ'.

On the other hand, organs of voluntary action must exist if there is to be spiritual experimentation and initiative. The complexity of our world needs not only the co-ordinating mind. It also needs the critical mind. The critic, by definition, is the agent of judgment. And by virtue of this role of judgment new experiments are initiated. These organs of voluntary action call for a rather different temperament and attitude.

These two organs of Christian witness and activity are not inimical to one another. Those engaged in them can respect each other and value each other's distinctive contribution. But they serve each other best by 'being in tension' *(ibid:*157).

The initiative-taking role of voluntarism is also stressed by Warren's colleague, Sir Kenneth Grubb, who was not only

President of CMS but also Chairman of the House of Laity in the National Assembly of the Church of England.

As I understand the New Testament, it is the duty, and ought to be the privilege of Christians to carry the Gospel to the uttermost parts of the earth . . . But our church as such did not do this: a few of its members did. Their hearts moved by the love of Christ, their wills united for a common good, and their intelligence quickened by the very obstacles they faced, they banded themselves together and set to work. They would have liked many bishops to bless them but they did not wait for this, knowing that good things often tarry (Taylor 1966:73).

John V. Taylor, Warren's successor as General Secretary of the CMS, reminds us that this initiative-taking genius of what he calls "the obedient nucleus" is not confined historically to evangelistic missions. And he makes the additional point that such vanguard groups, while sometimes praised in hindsight, are not welcomed as heroes initially.

However true it may be theologically that the whole Church is to be the servant of God and the Body of Christ in the world, in practice there has always been an obedient nucleus which carried the responsibility on behalf of the whole Church in a particular direction. For example, the whole Christian community ought to have been concerned in the matter of slavery in the eighteenth and nineteenth centuries; but in fact it was through the obedience of the Clapham Sect and other groups that the Church made its witness and exercised its healing ministry on that issue . . . It is worth remembering that the obedient nucleus, at least in its early days, has always seemed to be a lunatic fringe (ibid:75).

The concept of independence nowhere appears in these writings. On the contrary, they stress relatedness. Warren speaks of "intimate, though not necessarily constitutional, links . . . Links can be effective without being constitutional." This principle provides for voluntary societies across denominational lines in addition to one-communion, order-like societies such as CMS. Warren further sees the relationship of the two organs, in the Church and in society at large, as checks and balances against two opposing tendencies. On the one hand, unbridled initiative can degenerate into anarchy and be exploited by power-drunk individuals. But exploitation can equally come from power-hungry bureaucracies. The relational links holding organs of initiative and organs of cooperation together in creative tension safeguard the structures of society from being exploited by either extreme. "This is a fundamental principle of community . . . This has been the discovery of democracy at its best" (Warren 1974:158).

Here we must take leave of the history of voluntarism before I wear out my welcome. But we have certainly not written the last chapter. Further study needs to be done. For example, we have virtually ignored Germany and Scandinavia in the modern period. Here the Lutheran state churches which once resisted so tenaciously the emergence of committed communities, now accept them with an apparent minimum of tension. This is true of the nurturing chapels which are the spiritual children of Pietism's conventicles. It is also true of the outreaching mission societies, the majority of which have no organic connection with the official ecclesiastical bodies. It was the leaders of these very societies who stood strongly with Max Warren against the IMC-WCC merger, but to no avail. Yes, the relationships between church structures on the continent need further study.

In retrospect, we can now see both the Awakenings and the structural form of the new voluntary societies as equally the gifts of the Holy Spirit for buying up the unique missionary opportunities of a particular historical situation in the nineteenth century. And praise God, His people did not blow the game! These new sodalities provided a somewhat less intense but broader community experience than earlier models. Through financial contributions, committed Christians in the homelands felt deeply involved in the pioneer thrusts overseas.

Overseas missionaries found their sense of community gradually diluted by heterogeneity, individualism and increasing direction and control from the home boards. The latter moved gradually toward a business management model which focused on the appointment and direction of skilled individuals more than the development and enabling of communities of gifted people.

We could add that this trend has been further accentuated in the present century by allowing our increasingly-specialized mission staffs to get bogged down in institutions and church development. They almost *have* to be individually appointed — on the basis of their acquired skills — if we're to keep the schools and hospitals running, and fit others in where the now-established churches elect to use them. Paul & Co. didn't have that problem. They knew what their function was: to progressively move on and preach Christ where he was *not yet* named; or, in modern parlance, to *plant* churches — not to develop and develop and develop and develop them! Maybe if we were really clear on this distinction, we'd have less problem accepting the *separate* body-life of the mobile team vis-à-vis the local nurture structure it brings into being. When the former hangs around after the latter is clearly established, church/mission tensions are inevitable.

But much more importantly for our thesis, the resultant skills-oriented, individual appointments (to tasks which, quite often, we've drifted into) tend to smoke-screen even the plausibility, much less the *desirability,* of the gifts-oriented appointment of communal teams — for our *primary* missionary task of reaching the world's *un*reached peoples.

Well, our tour of historical models is over. Now we must push on to the history that we're currently walking through. As we do, we're aware that we're carrying with us an existing model, the voluntary society, that is still very much alive but ailing. And we're "stuck with" its infirmities. For while we're walking through an era of history in which change is so rapid that it is described by terms like "future shock", one sometimes feels that the only shocking thing happening within many of our mission structures is the relative absence of the kinds of change needed to adapt the model to today's challenges.

In some cases, this lack of up-dating tends to get concealed behind a certain technological modernity involving radio/TV, cassettes, aviation, visual aids, etc. This was a reasonably authentic form of up-dating in the 1940's (though, unfortunately, it contributed heavily to the specialization trend cited above). But as computer technology has illustrated, the "hardware" (with it's spinning disks and blinking lights) is not really "where it's at." Without the "software" of good programming, you have, as they say, GIGO — garbage in=garbage out.

If Carey were making his plea for "the use of means" *today,* he'd almost certainly include the "software" of the social sciences — building on anthropological insights about the perspectives and value systems of the world's many peoples as embodied in their cultures (their thought patterns, not just their languages); how these peoples make their decisions; and the cruciality of culture change which is so rampant in our day — providing extraordinary opportunities that call for extraordinary response. Happily, a growing emphasis on such software is occurring among leaders in the missionary establishment today.

But the most crucial question of all is: Whom will they lead? I now propose to turn from the software of history to the software of sociology as one of the key "means" we can use to answer that question. We need to understand what is happening to *us*. And when we do, we may well find that we need to rephrase our prayers. Instead of praying for men to match our mountains, we may need rather to pray for attractive structural vehicles to match our men — and women — whom, I believe, are already waiting in the wings. Join me as I try now to get to know them — to really know them.

CHAPTER 6

Commitment and Consciousness

Shifting from history to sociology is, perhaps, only shifting from "their" history to ours. So whatever view of history I hold applies to me as well as to them.

I mentioned earlier that I've been converted from a purely progressive view of history. I now realize that we do not necessarily make the best choices. We miss opportunities; we let the good slip through our fingers; we canonize outworn methods. In short, the "progress" of history looks much more like a chart of the Dow-Jones average than like a wheel chair ramp. Now I must apply all this to my — and our — lifetime, just as I have in looking at history "back there".

Actually, two forces are at work here. The tendency to assume that we have learned well from history, and have built on it progressively, is probably a product of our egos. But our insecurities are also at work. This causes us to particularly hang onto *our* history — the history we have known in our own lifetimes. They-don't-make-cars-like-they-used-to symbolizes more than mere nostalgia. While on the one hand we want to feel we've improved on the past, we also can feel threatened about others improving on our performance. In our better moments we want our children to excel us, but not all our moments are better moments! This can be relatively harmless nostalgia if we limit our mutterings to half-truths about Detroit dinosaurs. If need be, we can expose such generalizations to hard data. Come to think of it, my

11-year-old, 140,000-mile Pontiac is doing better than any previous car I've owned.

Commitment in Time and Culture

But when we shift from the quality of cars to the quality of commitment, we're dealing with something far more subjective — and more important. It is of particular importance to those of us who consider ourselves committed. Yet we are subject to the same, often-unconscious ambivalence cited above: we want to see this commitment reproduced in our spiritual children, but we feel threatened by commitment which takes a different *form* than ours. We may even fail to recognize it as commitment.

This ambivalence is complicated by the tendency of Christians to think about commitment primarily as an absolute or biblical value. For example, we tend to preach missionary commitment from the Bible. But we don't get far before we start citing historical illustrations from William Carey to Jim Elliot. Why? Simply because commitment as a value or attitude is of little practical consequence until it is expressed. And expression requires some form of expression. We are more apt to cite Jim Elliot's (or John and Betty Stam's) commitment than that of Francis of Assisi; for the form in which Jim lived out his commitment fits, at least idealistically, our own frame of reference. No problem so far. We all work from our personal frames of reference. The problem enters when we fail to recognize that our preferred or idealized form of expression (based on our frame of reference) and the basic biblical value are not the same thing. The former is an application of the latter. And the former is influenced by our environment.

In other words, commitment doesn't happen either in a vacuum or an idealized environment. Even our initial commitment to Jesus Christ, a very intimate personal relationship, must be worked out against a backdrop of the real world. So much more will our further commitments as Christians — to our brethren and to the task — relate to the history we walk through. Even the most idealized commitment will be affected by the tenor of the times — what the Germans call *Zeitgeist*.

As an example, note how today's *Zeitgeist* affects the career commitments of young adults. Most of them make their career decisions later than we did. They also make them more tentatively.

And who can blame them? Had Alvin Toffler never written *Future Shock*, they could still observe this phenomenon for themselves. Many of them saw their highly-trained and experienced fathers cut adrift in mid-career by the obsoleting "improvements" of technology. Space engineers replace aeronautical engineers. Computers replace people. And even "national" churchmen replace missionaries. Once again we're looking at part-truths. In the latter case, if you define the word missionary accurately, the truth portion of the statement is small indeed. But that's beside the point here. We're discussing how commitment is affected by the *Zeitgeist*: the trend of thought and feeling in a period (Webster's 1966). And we're discussing this in order to understand it — not to excuse it. Neither the devil nor the *Zeitgeist* makes us settle for stunted commitment. We can do that quite well on our own.

Yes, the committed must eventually commit — against the tide. But if I made a second-decision commitment at age 15, and, due to the *Zeitgeist* (or any other reason), my son makes a similar commitment at age 25, he is not thereby 40% less committed, or less spiritual. Furthermore, the form of his commitment may look so different from mine that I either assign it a lower value or fail to recognize it altogether. In reality, his commitment may be even stronger and more valid in relationship to his world. But my feelings are subject to that ambivalent threat of being improved upon, as discussed earlier.

Yet something more seems to be going on here. Is my son affected by a different *Zeitgeist* than mine? The definition quoted above talks about the thought and feeling trends of a "period", but the Shorter Oxford Dictionary (Third Edition, 1964) adds a key word: "the thought or feeling peculiar to a generation or period." Ah, here's something that those of us who watched our kids become adults in the 60's can understand: that famous generation gap. According to this second definition we can apparently have more than one *Zeitgeist* around at the same time. This certainly is the view of Charles Reich in his best-selling, controversial *Greening of America* (1971). He prefers the term "consciousness" and identifies three of them in the current scene. His Consciousness III, which we associate mostly with the younger generation, is more frequently cited by others than the distinction between his two older categories of consciousness.

A New Consciousness; A New Era

Reich is not alone in his view of a multiple-*Zeitgeist*. But more commonly a two-fold paradigm is suggested. Philip Slater (1971) talks about old-culture and new-culture. Roszak (1969) uses the term counter-culture to designate the new. What an anthropologist calls a culture usually involves a more homogeneous people; and their body of shared ideas is normally more extensive and integrated. Thus we can attribute a culture to Navaho society, but if we're talking about American society we more properly speak of a *Zeitgeist* — or a consciousness. We'll find all these terms useful as we seek relevant current application of our historical models for commitment, community, and the combination of the two. But I will most frequently adapt Reich's choice and speak of the emerging or new consciousness. This term is broader than culture, and therefore more descriptive of what I feel is happening.

At any rate, these authors have this in common: they are clearly convinced that they are dealing with more than a gap (generational or communicational alone) or a fad. Franklin Murphy, former Chancellor of the University of California at Los Angeles, makes the same point, though he comes at it from a unique angle.

> Society and the university accepted and were directed in the 17th and 18th centuries by the statement of Descartes, *Cognito ergo sum* — "I think, therefore I am." . . . Thus was ushered in the so-called age of reason.
>
> In the 19th century, as a major by-product of the Industrial Revolution, a new concept was introduced —*Facio ergo sum* — "I do, therefore I am." And so materialism, the production, possession and distribution of goods and services became a guiding principle . . . Now, in our times, economic affluence has been achieved (at least for the majority of our society), and yet it is clear to an increasing number of people that economic affluence did not lead to nirvana but to a cul-de-sac . . .
>
> Now it is my view that at this point in history, and probably well into the twenty-first century, the philosophical leitmotiv may well become *Sentio ergo sum* — "I feel, therefore I am." . . . Herein lies, I believe, one of the major inputs to the so-called generation gap (1968).

Note that Murphy is not talking about decades, generations or even centuries. He is talking about eras. If in fact the emerging consciousness is based on such an era change, we are faced with a very large change indeed. More than ever we should not be surprised if we find that the expression, form and timing of commitment varies from one consciousness to another.

Yet one factor almost certainly will not change: the wide spectrum of commitment *levels* we've noted in earlier chapters. For this is related to humanness rather than consciousness. And for the same reason, we'll find that the deeper levels of commitment are present in only a relatively small minority. When the new consciousness surfaced with high visibility in the late 60's, we saw one minority in action (though the media coverage gave the impression that much larger numbers were involved). Probably only a minority of that minority had a real commitment to the causes for which they marched and chanted. Oh, they all had a concern. In fact, this concern extended, in varying degrees, even to the majority who stayed in the dorms. But certainly many of the marchers had only a tentative or temporary commitment. And some were only "committed" to venting their feelings.

These tumultous days had to pass. Historically, counter-cultures build a reservoir of tension before surfacing. Some of the steam has to be released. But even the most dedicated radicals cannot live that way long term. Today the drop-out is the most visible left-over of those earlier heady days, and do-your-own-thing has become a new hedonism for many. Yet if we look only at this low-commitment side of the movement, we are doing a disfavor not only to the generation but to ourselves. Here and there we find scattered press stories today of young professionals choosing to work in non-profit medical clinics and legal aid services for the poor. They found their post-frustration ways to express their commitment. We need some nose-counting research on how many of yesterday's protest leaders are so involved. We might be surprised. But even so, the number will be small, percentage-wise. It always has been.

Alongside these scattered news stories of channeled commitment, the media more often gives us generalized coverage of the campus scene today. The typical, cliche-like "depth" story compares the activists of the late 60's with today's students who are industriously pursuing professional training for high-salary-producing careers. There is no doubt truth in the latter trend, but the comparison distorts the picture. For it compares yesterday's apples with today's bananas. The "straight" students studying for traditional careers were there all the time but quite covered up by the press' temporary love affair with the headline-and-copy-producing "freaks". Now the emphasis on the growing number who seemingly have no quarrel with "the system" distorts the total picture in the opposite direction. And even to the degree that these stories are accurate, they do not reflect the campus scene as much as they reflect the nature of today's media, which is also a highly-competitive business that must merchandise its product. In the absence of headline-producing conflict, we are treated to the kind of news we want to hear: if our children now look more like us we are soothed and gratified; our values are vindicated.

Once again, we as well as our successors will be the losers if we are lulled by this kind of shallow reporting. Responsible, committed Christians interested in the future of missionary outreach must necessarily focus on what *is,* including what remains from the more visible 60's, rather than contentedly tabulating what seems to have disappeared. The new consciousness has, after all, grown out of the old. It could not possibly be different in its entirety. The similarities naturally exceed the distinctives. The former we can handle with relative ease; coping with the latter is our challenge. And we will only truly cope with the distinctives of the new consciousness as we approach them with a primary desire to understand them rather than to rebut them. Understanding does not require agreement; but it does require openness, and, ideally, empathy.

Alternative Life Styles

Our immediate (but not exclusive) concern is to understand the effect of the new consciousness on commitment, including the forms it is apt to take. And since we are examining this group consciousness as somewhat of a sub-culture, what, if any, are its *shared* commitments? At the beginning of his final chapter, Reich asks what he calls the most important question concerning the new consciousness: how permanent is it? Then he deals with current views (at the turn of the decade) of what is happening. He describes the views of the liberals, "many blacks and many spokesmen for the poor," the New Left, and even Marcuse as "woefully inadequate."

> Moreover, almost none of the views we have mentioned recognizes the crucial importance of *choosing a new life-style.* This has been passed

over as if it were no more than an indulgent product of affluence . . .
But choice of a life style is not peripheral, it is the heart of the new
awakening (1971:380, emphasis by Reich).

Granted, this kind of sweeping statement is one of the things
Reich's critics faulted; and I can agree with them — in part. But I
cannot, on that basis, sweep him under the rug. And this particular
quote illustrates why. For the evidence in 1976 points toward a
vindication of his forecast that choice of life-style is one of the more
permanent signs of the new consciousness.

The first thing we're dealing with here is choice. Choice is not the
same thing as commitment, but it is related. Of course, it could be
argued that for the children of the middle class (which form the core
of the new consciousness), more choice is available today than at
any previous time in history. But is that really true? Most of us who
took up our careers after moth-balling our WWII uniforms have had
some viable choices during the past 30 years. We did not have to join
the inexorable "rise" to security to suburbia to status. Yet how many
dropped out of that rat race of their own volitional choice? The
number is so small that it is virtually invisible. We pursued this
apparently upward path (without really thinking about it) as far as
we could — until our limitations of ability or circumstances topped
us out. We may not have reached affluence by our definition, but
this lack was not a matter of choice. For many of our children it is.

Conscious choice is usually better than drift. But there's no
guarantee that the choices of today's young will always come out
"good". We've noted self-indulgent life-style choices, at the
drop-out end of the spectrum, that differ from the old playboy
hedonism only in style. We have also noted those students, that the
media tends to focus on today, who seem to be opting for a life style
that looks a lot like ours. The latter may be "good" in some cases;
"bad" in others. But between these two edges of the new
consciousness, large numbers of relatively-quiet young adults are
consciously choosing a simpler, less-materialistic life style. The
degree of simplicity varies widely, even in this centrist segment. So
does the degree to which consumerism is avoided. But there are still
some reasonably common denominators or symbols.

Some indicators, of course, point to the fact that the bulk of the
new consciousness is as consumption-oriented as the old. If anyone
wants to establish this premise, he might start by surveying the

apartments of these young people and noting their stereo systems, some of which are quite elaborate. True, these cost a lot of money. They also are direct products of that technocratic society which the counter-culture is specifically opposed to (Roszak 1969:sub-title). But this is not as inconsistent as it seems at first glance. In the first place, as Reich accurately points out, the new consciousness "does not reject technique,* it rejects domination by technique" (1971:388). Beyond this, we must recognize that the stereo system, along with the TV set, does not symbolize materialism or technology as much as it symbolizes media. The electronic technology of these media represents continuity with the old consciousness; the *use* of these media represents discontinuity. For us, music is primarily entertainment; for them it is primarily communication (or, to follow McLuhan, message). This is even more graphically illustrated in the electronic amplification of instrument and voice in their musical "groups".

But there are other indicators that clearly point to the simpler life style. Take for instance that ultimate symbol of American technology, the automobile. Again, we see nothing like total rejection among the young. Even many drop-outs manage ownership, often communally, of an elderly beat-up van. At the other end of the spectrum, the career-conscious student may get more than transportation from his Porsche; he may get the same identity crutch from it that his materially-successful but insecure dad gets from his Continental. Between these two, some new things are happening.

For twelve years I've lived between one of California's oldest community colleges and the State University at Fullerton. The campuses are only two miles apart and now have a combined enrollment of more than 30,000. When it comes to external criteria like transportation, I can practically research the student generation from my doorstep! Here in auto-oriented Southern California, the campus parking lots have grown steadily with the enrollment. The fact that the VW bug has been the most prominent student vehicle

---

* Here Reich employs the term Jacques Ellul popularized in his *The Technological Society* (1964), a book which Roszak refers to, apparently with admiration, as an "outrageously pessimistic book [which] is thus far the most global effort to depict the technocracy in full operation" (1969:6).

can hardly be cited as a sign of simplicity. But the revival of the bicycle can. This two-wheel resurgence began with the ecological emphasis early in this decade, but the real revolution came in 1973 with the fuel crisis. More importantly, it came to stay. The canvas or nylon book bag on the cyclist's back is as much a symbol today as the wandering hippie's knapsack and bed roll were in the 60's. The energy crisis also brought, at long last, some improved public transportation to Southern California. And today, those sidewalk benches at the bus stops are occupied by more under-30's than over-70's.

Admittedly, these particular life-style symbols do not represent a majority. But once again, commitment levels always vary widely, and the deeper levels involve a small, but far from insignificant minority.

A somewhat broader new life style value (it hardly qualifies as a commitment) that I find particularly interesting involves clothing. Back in Chaper 4 I quoted Littell's comment on the culturally-primitivistic tendencies of the Hutterites in modern times. He noted that their valued plain clothes had become peculiar clothes. The exact opposite has happened in our youth generation: freak clothes have become plain clothes. (And, as with the Hutterites, the clothing style itself is not primarily what has changed.) In the 60's it was popular to scoff at the big style switch which purported to be an expression of do-your-own-thing. We were quick to point out that it had merely become a new uniform. No doubt that was at least partly true. But today one would have to be middle-class beyond all redemption to attribute the omnipresent jeans and T-shirts primarily to this follow-the-leader phenomenon. Style simply does not matter that much to a large number — possibly even a majority — of the young. The fact that most young people still have some dressier clothes and wear them on occasion does not negate this view. On the contrary, it underscores the fact that the plain clothes are no longer a protest but a preference. And as such, they may be the most potent symbol that a simpler life style is one continuing value of the new consciousness. But as always, this is expressed in varying degrees.

Commitment to Life Style

As we shift our focus to Christians within the new consciousness, we see some evidence that simpler life styles involve more than a value; for many it is a clear commitment. This is reflected in the kind of jobs they seek — and those they avoid. Also books are now appearing on the subject (e.g. Eller 1973; Gish 1973; Taylor 1975). For Gish the simple life is not just a commitment to a duty. His first chapter (p. 23ff.) is entitled "How to Spend Less and Enjoy it More." And he is not alone in the conviction that there is more joy in simplicity than in material comfort. With obvious irony, Reich titles a chapter about the plasticity of existing American values, "It's Just Like Living." Even secular analysts see this value of the simple life.

But Gish is also interested in a deeper commitment. "Voluntary poverty . . . can give power and authenticity to our lives. In a new way, we can capture the best vision of the Roman Catholic orders" (1973:24). He is not suggesting, of course, that we imitate the actual life styles of the monks. It is rather clear that even the relatively primitivist devotees of the simple life today would not be attracted to those austere early monasteries in Ireland, as the young men of that day were. But then, life in Ireland was bleak and hard for nearly everyone. The alternative life style of the Irish monks involved a variety of voluntary austerities of which poverty may have been the least significant. But simplicity was involved. Furthermore, as we noted in Chapter 3 the Irish monasteries, in contrast to the Egyptian/Continental movement, were less inclined to turn their backs on their rich cultural heritage along with their flesh-world-devil denial. They wedded joy and deep commitment in an extremely simple life.

So did Francis of Assisi. This is a more apt illustration of what Gish is citing, and more appropriate to today's overall *Zeitgeist*. For in his pursuit of the simple life, Francis dropped out of the newly-affluent mercantile society of thirteenth century northern Italy. Interestingly, his counter-cultural life style of extreme simplicity and poverty attracted many committed youth. Yet within a very few years, many members of even this strongly-committed minority found the idealistic life style too extreme. They were still committed to the same general principles, but agitated for moderation of the *degree* of austerity. Thus began the dissentions over the Rule that have plagued and splintered the Franciscan Order ever since. In spite of this, the contributions of the Franciscans are legendary. There is room, it would seem, for various levels of application; commitment to the simple life need not be extreme to be valid.

Actually, all the committed community models we examined in Chapters 3 and 4 had a life-style element in common. As in the case of the Irish, and also the Hutterites and Moravians, this did not necessarily place the primary emphasis on the level of economic austerity (though that was normally present to some degree). But all these committed groups chose alternate life styles that significantly broke with the various easy values of their surrounding societies. It is because of this common thread running through our historical models — which we must eventually relate to our current *Zeitgeist* — that I have dwelt at length on the life-style trend within the new consciousness.

The Jesus Movement

Touching base again with those more visible years when this new consciousness emerged, we ought to comment specifically on the Christian young people who, by and large, evidenced the strongest commitment to an alternate life style. Like Gish, they saw more joy and meaning in the simple life. But they reached back beyond the Orders for a model. "A man's real life in no way depends upon the number of his possessions" (Luke 12:15, Phillips). This is certainly one reason why they are properly known as Jesus people. They could also identify with Jesus' description of *his* life style: "Foxes have holes and the birds of the air have nests, but the Son of Man has nowhere to lay his head" (Luke 9:58). For in those days they, along with their non-Christian counterparts, were known as street people.

Call to the Streets is the personal saga of Don Williams (1972), highly-credentialed young churchman: ordained Presbyterian youth pastor with a Ph.D. His introduction to the world of the streets, through a teen-age convert, provides an instructive backward look from the perspective of 1975.

> Cheryl took me to the streets. The summer of 1967 found the hippie world in full swing. I discovered Hollywood Boulevard and the Sunset Strip only blocks from the church building which had served as an effective buffer between myself and the surrounding community. It was a swirling world of bizarre dress and bizarre behavior. "Love" and "peace," ideals that too often only meant sex

and drugs, still expressed genuine longings. By their outlandish costumes and freaky hair these "flower children" were not only "putting down" the technological society and social ladder of suburbia, but also crying out to be recognized as real persons, unique individuals. They called each other "beautiful," looking for that inner beauty of which the Bible so often speaks, rather than the status symbols of a manipulated mass society.

I was rightly impressed with the honest, engaging conversations that were possible in the "hip" world. No longer did I have to watch my dress and monitor my words, carefully looking for the opportunity to speak of Christ, as I had done in the fraternities and sororities on the campus. Here all was wide open. My first conversation with Cheryl and her roommate Michelle covered everything from God, sex, parents, the Bible, drugs, church, and the future in rapid-fire conversation. Was I a virgin? (I was.) Had I done drugs? (I hadn't.) Was Christ real to me? (He was.) Elements of this conversation were repeated again and again that summer. My defenses began to go. I was either honest or out. There were no alternatives.

God used Cheryl to teach me many things in the great process of setting me free. One week after I met her she came again to church, rushed across the patio, threw her arms around me and gave me a big kiss. For a young, unmarried minister who had avoided any hint of scandal, I was stunned. I felt as if my head were turning 360 degrees looking for the church's elders, while every muscle in my body froze. Later in reflection on this incident I realized that Cheryl was only being her street self. I further realized that while I talked about Christian freedom, Cheryl actually was much more free than I. It was a new world indeed that I was entering.

I began to listen to that world. I saw its notorious underground papers, felt its anarchic and escapist spirit, heard the false promises of its hallucinogenic drugs, and saw the influx of Eastern religion offer a new spirituality to Western minds fed up with pragmatism and materialism. I reeled under its biting criticism of racism and war. I blushed at the silence of the church and fought the temptation to become defensive. My deepest listening came at the point of its music. Here I began to feel the full weight of the cultural revolution, and here I found a great secret: music is the key to this generation because music is the one place in the mass media where kids editorialize to kids (1972:21-23).

That was 1967. Nine years have passed. (In some ways it seems more like two decades.) Mid-way to the present, in 1971, a spate of books appeared on the Jesus people. Reviewing these analyses today provides further perspective. Billy Graham gave the young people high marks: "The vast majority of them are genuine in their commitment . . . The movement, thus far, centers in Jesus . . . The movement is Bible-based" (1971:16,17).

> The burden that the Jesus kids feel for others is real. There are tears of joy when someone confesses Jesus. They pray with agony for the kids they know on the streets. They love with a rescuing kind of love. Jesus is not just a nice idea. He is real, and they see him meeting people right where they are, on the streets (Palms 1971:19).

But these new Christians were not that warm toward the traditional churches. On this point, all the writers agree. Enroth and his co-authors are possibly the most established-church oriented of the lot — to the point of rather looking down their rationalistic noses at the simplicity (and simplistic trends) of the movement. Yet they begin their conclusion with:

> Whatever one's final opinion of the Jesus People is, their existence is a searing indictment of a desiccated, hidebound institutional church. Until the Jesus People phenomenon occured, the church as a whole had almost completely ignored the young people of the counter-culture, except for occasional denunciation of them as typical examples of the decadence of our times . . .

> To the counter-culture, the established church appeared as a comfortable middle-class ghetto of mutual admirers who damned the rest of the world, complacently approved the status quo, and felt no need for a radical critique of the materialism and decadence of American society. Their coming to Christ has not changed their opinion of the established church (Enroth 1972:240).

Ed Plowman is another committed churchman who sensed this problem, as reflected in the title of the first edition of his book on the movement, *The Underground Church.*

> I recall in the early days of the movement how Arthur Blessitt all but wept into the telephone as he told of pastors turning away new converts he had sent . . . That kind of rejection is rare today. Instead of being turned away, converts are being turned off . . . What they really want is involvement in a dynamic community of faith where Jesus is not shut out by tradition-encrusted forms and agendas (1971:122).

Another common denominator of these early-in-the-decade

books is a question phrased in various forms: Fad or faith? Will it last? What's the future of the movement? That, of course, was the question we all had. Almost without realizing it, most of those authors pointed to the next phase of the movement when they reported that at the time of their writing, these young people were reaching out for teaching.

> Francis Cook, pastor of Calvary Baptist Church in Saginaw, Michigan, went to a Jesus people's meeting. He wanted to find out what the Jesus movement is all about. Because he went to them, instead of waiting for them to come to his church, they were responsive to him. When they found out that he believed the teachings of the Bible and taught it as God's Word, they asked him to be their Bible teacher. "We can lead them to Christ," they told him, "but we need a Bible teacher." . . . He has found a whole new dimension of ministry because he has made himself available to the kids. They are what every teacher dreams about, a people who want to learn. And he does not make them "go get a haircut" (Palms 1971:87).

> Firm, even dogmatic, biblical teachings do not offend the Jesus kids. "Tell it straight," they say . . . But the dogma must be biblical, not cultural. The Jesus kids know very well that some of the churches that pride themselves in being "Bible centered" are not Bible centered at all. They preach about a saved soul and ignore the real business of belonging to, and following, Jesus Christ. The Jesus kids want the teachings of the Bible, not the teachings of an institution that is more influenced by the cultural and social drives of its members than it is by the discipleship and Christian life-style taught in the Bible (ibid:91).

Billy Graham echoes this last evaluation: "The emphasis in this movement is on Christian discipleship" (1971:19).

The New Consciousness Today

Five years later, discipleship training is very much "where it's at." And this process is taking place in a wide variety of settings: in those communities and residential houses of the movement that have survived; in continuing ministries to the sub-culture such as the Christian World Liberation Front of Berkeley; in specific training ministries spawned by the movement such as the Jesus Christ Light & Power Company of Los Angeles; but most of all, in local churches. Yes, these former street Christians have been entering regularly-organized churches. But not just any kind. Very often the particular churches they migrate to are Pentecostal in background, but not just any Pentecostal church either — indicating that the style of the church is probably more crucial than its doctrinal distinctives. The churches that attract them are first and foremost made up of accepting people; their style of worship is marked by openness, freedom and joy; the teaching is authoritative, consequential and personally applicable. The best known example is Calvary Chapel of Santa Ana (sometimes erroneously given as Costa Mesa), California, which now has a Sunday morning attendance of over 6000 in 3 services.

We see the same thing happening here that happened within the counter-culture as a whole: reservoir of tension, break-through with high visibility, exhilaration or euphoria, slowdown to a more livable pace, reassessment of strategy toward the realistic and attainable. A lot of this process is unconscious and triggered by real-life factors such as fatigue, disappointment, need, marriage and family, etc. In any new movement, of course, some will become so discouraged by the latter factors that the dream fades and the goals are abandoned. But that is an entirely different matter than the more normal, even inevitable, slowdown and reassessment process. This expected process does not usually signal the disappearance of a movement, but rather a redirection of its creative energy. It must be admitted that it's not always easy to tell which process is taking place: redirection or abandonment. But I have seen enough current vitality to take that risk gladly.

There is yet another reason, beyond this slowing-down-to-learn process, why the movement is less visible today. Like any historical movement, the Jesus people phenomenon had several streams. The high-visibility Christian street scene we have been discussing is important because of its unique relationship to the counter-culture. But just as we have viewed the new consciousness as broader than the counter-culture, the new consciousness among Christians is broader than any one stream of the Jesus movement. TIME's landmark cover story in June of 1971 was titled "The Jesus Revolution," which implied something even broader than the youth scene. Consistent with this, the article identified several revolutionary streams, though it concentrated primarily on the first.

The JESUS PEOPLE, also known as Street Christians or Jesus Freaks, are the most visible . . . THE STRAIGHT PEOPLE, by far the largest

group, are mainly active in interdenominational, evangelical campus
and youth movements . . . (TIME 1971:59).

When this story appeared, I felt the editors were mixing apples and
oranges to include the existing campus groups. They even included
the Catholic Pentecostals as a third stream. I could see how the latter
fitted into the "revolution" theme of that article more easily than I
could see the presence there of the straight students. At least that
was my view in mid-1971.

In hindsight, I basically agree with Robert Ellwood who wrote
12-18 months behind the 1971-72 books we've been quoting from.
"The Jesus movement did not begin on the campus, but it caught on
there almost immediately" (1973:112). Immediately? Well, at least it
wasn't long before the consciousness or *Zeitgeist* was affecting large
numbers of students who still appeared relatively straight. They felt
some of the same disaffections that were being acted out by their
peers on the streets, though probably to a lesser degree. However,
they did not have the same felt need to vocalize or dramatize their
concerns so forcefully.

From a 1976 perspective, many of these "centrist" young adults
appear as the most promising heirs of the overall movement. From
their number, most of tomorrow's committed participants — and
tomorrow's leadership — will probably arise. But interspersed with
them (both participants and leaders) will almost certainly be some of
yesterday's true Jesus "freaks". And we may never know the
difference. Even today they study and worship together in campus
groups (IVCF, CCC, Navs), in house churches, and in established
congregations. (In the latter, they are often more related to a
grouping of their peers than to the congregation as a whole.) This
adds to the illusion that the movement has "gone straight".

The terms straight and freak are actually quite inappropriate (and
no longer appreciated) today — though still somewhat descriptive
of smaller groupings at each pole of the youth generation. At the one
pole, groups like the Children of God have moved deeper into their
enclosures and will probably never realize the creative contribution
they might have made, as have other "lunatic fringe" groups in
history. At the other pole, of course, are the mild to meek. This is
true of every generation, and these brothers and sisters should not
be despised. At the same time, we know that creativity does not
arise from this segment — and strong commitment only rarely. Yet

we will be less than human if we are not at least tempted to anoint them as our successors. Because it is only human to evaluate our progeny primarily in terms of how much they look like us.

We are back to where we started this chapter: noting the difficulty each generation faces in evaluating the quality of commitment in its children. For commitment finds expression in terms of the current environment, and each generation must respond to the particular piece of history that it walks through. This natural process has been accentuated since 1960 by an above-average change in the younger generation's frame of reference, which may well represent a major era change. We must understand something of the resultant new mass consciousness, or *Zeitgeist,* if we are to understand the forms of commitment that are valid for young adults today.

In looking for shared values or commitment within this new consciousness, we noted a deliberate move toward alternate life styles. While this trend involved some elements of protest or rejection, the alternates were embraced by purposeful choice. Some of the chosen alternates hardly stimulate applause; some involve little real change. But there is a growing trend among many to choose a simpler life style geared to reduced consumption. The degree of reduction varies widely. Some Christian young people have not only followed this trend but have elevated the choice to a commitment, motivated by biblical models, particularly the life of Jesus.

The Jesus people dramatized, and contributed to, this kind of Christian commitment. In its maturing process, this movement has fostered and uncovered additional areas of commitment among the young: to the Bible as the Word of God; to serious study of the Bible; and to Christian discipleship. We must explore further the heritage of this movement in its broadened scope. Right now, we shall do this in the context of another of its growing (but still tentative) commitments: to community.

CHAPTER 7

Community

As we've noted, anthropologists refer to tribal and village people as "face to face" societies. The West in general, and America in particular, clearly does not qualify for that category. We might more properly be called the bumper to bumper society!

Some people, like Harvey Cox, view the demise of village face-to-faceness as good riddance. In fact, he asks us to "celebrate" the Secular City (1966). I, for one, have to decline his invitation. At the same time, I must recognize both urbanization and secularization as facts of life. While I don't see these facts as something to sing about, I do view them as a challenge I must cope with. And Cox, for all his theological nonsense and anthropological naiveté, does offer some practical common sense on which to build such coping skills.

He reminds us that it's easy to look back at the pre-urban ethos with a naive nostalgia — and confuse it with the Christian concept of *koinonia*. In reality, the involuntary togetherness of village life can also be depersonalizing, even vicious. Then borrowing Buber's terminology, he asks us to be realistic about how many people we can have an intimate I-Thou relationship with, in any kind of society. Consequently, we must put some people who cross our lives into a lesser category — or we won't have adequate time to develop our deeper relationships. Even the Good Samaritan didn't form an I-Thou relationship with the thieves' victim. But neither did he treat him as an "It". Cox suggests that Buber's philosophy suffers from an unnecessary dichotomy. He proposes an intermediate I-*You* category for "all those public relationships we so enjoy in the city but which we do not allow to develop into private ones. These contacts can be decidedly human even though they remain somewhat distant" *(ibid*:39-42). Cox's point is well taken. The depth to which we can develop our really personal relationships depends on their number.

The same can be said about the development of a community. Broader fellowship can be extended indefinitely by means of community-to-community links. But within any one community, some limitation must be placed on size, by whatever criteria or device. We noted all this earlier in Chapter 1. Of course, limited size will not, of itself, produce community. But it's a place to start. To make this possible, we must accept the fact that a merely I-You public relationship with most of the people on our block is not sinful. And, dare I say it? — the same applies to most of the people in our urban congregation. When we accept this, we can relax and commit ourselves to a realistic number of people in true community.

Committed to One Another

That *is* an essential ingredient of community: commitment to one another. In fact, for the kind of community we are discussing in this chapter, this mutual commitment lays the groundwork. We must stop short, though, of viewing mutual commitment as "foundational." For people are not even drawn together into such community unless they have a strongly shared outlook or idealism in the first place. For a secular community, this common foundation may be a commitment to a more humane society. For a truly Christian community, the only authentic foundation is personal commitment to Jesus Christ.

At this point, I want to make a clear distinction between this commitment to an outlook (or to Christ), on the one hand, and commitment to a *task* on the other. The first is foundational to community; the other is a potential product of community. Now to put the whole picture together, I see a three-commitment process. In the Christian context: 1) our commitment to Christ is the indispensable foundation; 2) a community is formed by our commitment to one another; and 3) we express our original (foundational) commitment *in* community by way of a shared commitment to a task. The order is crucial — crucial, that is, to committed Christian community. There are, of course, other ways of living and serving. But our present subject is community (in a more committed framework than our usage of this word at the beginning of Chapter 1). To illustrate the importance of this order, let's make various changes in it and see what happens.

In the 60's, some (but not all) of the secular communes that emerged were made up of true drop-outs. They had little or no constructive commitment to society and admitted it. Their resultant communal life styles could hardly be termed communities. They were, rather, collections of hedonistic individuals; each person was committed primarily to himself.

More commonly, we find basically dedicated people commiting themselves to a task, and then gathering with or enlisting others who are concerned with the same cause. This is essentially what happened in nineteenth-century voluntarism. As we've seen, the resulting voluntary societies fitted that *Zeitgeist* and brought about tremendous accomplishments. This is still a valid form of commitment to Christian (or other) activism today. But such joint enterprises should not be confused with community, even though, as we have recognized, community may occasionally occur in this context as a third step.

As a third illustration, we all know people whose lives seem *primarily* dedicated to a task. The archetype is the business or professional man who is so wedded to his chosen work that he cannot even maintain horizontal relationships with his own family — and certainly has no time for God. He has gone straight to commitment number three. At times we see something similar to this in a Christian minister — or in poor Betty's "senior missionary"! Such people do, of course, have a commitment to Christ, but their one-sided, excessive commitment to a specific *task* may actually cover up an immature, or distorted, primary commitment. Furthermore, for both Christian and non-Christian alike, this order of commitment is only an extreme manifestation of what Franklin Murphy was talking about when he spoke of the emphasis within our established consciousness as *facio ergo sum,* "I do (or make or produce), therefore I am." It is this kind of cultural effect on the whole concept of commitment that necessitates our present discussion.

Caring, Sharing Groups

This latter illustration also pinpoints the peculiar importance of community in our society today — a society deeply in need of a return to authentic relationships. For some, this has become a felt need. And some of these, in turn, are doing something about it. In Christian circles, a considerable relational literature has appeared, authored by men like Bruce Larson, Keith Miller and Lyman Coleman. Commitment to one another in small groups is a recurring theme in this literature. Since the people who make up such caring, sharing groups are generally committed to Christ, we see true, though often temporary, communities in operation here (commitments one and two). Stephen Clark, the Catholic renewal community leader we met earlier, looks beyond the very small group and calls for medium-size Christian communities within parishes and congregations that have generally become too large for true community (1972).

We are talking here, of course, about problems in our society which call for new forms of Christian nurture. That's a little off the subject of our book, since we are concentrating on the other structure of the Church, the sodality. But what we see happening in this relational movement is instructive to our community theme — and also our commitment theme, for that matter. Elton Trueblood, one of the earliest and ablest of the relational authors, calls one of his books, *The Company of the Committed* (1961). He, too, calls for spiritually elite communities, in the midst of nominalism, as a renewing force.

Finley Edge takes this one step further and discusses small groups within the congregation in terms of "come" structures and "go" structures (1971:163). In so doing, he partly reflects the two-structure nature of the Church right in the local setting. This also suggests that some of the emerging structures of the relational movement may yet become the kind of fully committed communities we are primarily concerned with in this book.

Not all these caring, relational groups are forming wholly within existing congregations. A great many of them are quite independent of the official congregational program, though many of these, in turn, are supplemental rather than competitive. In other words, the members of these groups are searching for a more relevant faith which is too often hidden in the archaic forms of our established churches.

This trend is a repetition of the conventicles or *ecclesiolae* ("little churches") of the Pietist movement that we met in Chapter 4. The people involved (then and now) still are members of and attend their regular churches. But since they often find more meaningful worship, in addition to a stronger fellowship, in the less-structured supplemental community, the probability is high that some of these groups will eventually become regular congregations. The clergy (and hierarchy) of existing congregations often tend to look on this phenomenon as the tragic divisiveness of elitism. This view avoids facing up to the indictment of existing congregations that is implicit in the current trends. Viewed more positively, the supplemental communities (now and in history) are necessary agencies of renewal. Where the existing structures respond, in any reasonable degree, to this renewing force, the small communities will probably continue their supplemental function only. But even where new congregations eventuate, we ought not view this as tragedy; it is, after all, a form of growth by multiplication.

But, of course, some of these less-structured communities of healing and nurture, stressing a caring-sharing commitment to one another, are clearly not supplemental: they are, rather, *alternatives* to the existing local churches. This category of new communities will soon bring us back to the Jesus movement and the new consciousness. But to this point, the caring communities we have been speaking of are much more prominent among the older or existing consciousness. I don't feel that I can stress too strongly the importance of this fact. For here is the strongest sort of evidence that the new consciousness we have been discussing does not involve only the simple addition of a *Zeitgeist* (as implied by Reich's Roman numerals); the overall *Zeitgeist* is, in fact, changing. To the young, this change seems painfully slow; for many others, it is a source of regret. But for all planners and decision makers — most especially, Christian decision makers who care about the acceleration of sharing our saving faith with a lost world — this change had just better be taken seriously!

The Jesus People and Community

Even the clearly alternative nurture communities are found

among people no longer classifiable as young. Some contain a healthy age mixture. But we need to look briefly now at the incidence of such communities among the new consciousness, per se. We noted in the previous chapter that the most visible Jesus people, the street Christians, are now largely involved in discipleship training. We noted that this maturation and growth is, for many, taking place in established congregations of a certain type. Others have sought out Bible teachers to train them in their own alternative communities.

When we talk about communities among these people, our thoughts are apt to shift to communal living situations. For this was a definite part of the Jesus people scene circa 1970. But as we look back on that period, it is clear that those particular Christian houses were a relatively temporary, though interesting, phenomenon. The urban houses provided an ideal environment for an accepting community of young Christians to "rap", over a several-day period, with visitors who were genuine seekers; i.e. relational evangelism geared to the then counter-culture. Other communities, in rural settings, provided an important drug-free Christian environment for new Christians needing this kind of rehabilitation. Beyond these specialized objectives (which are still functioning in some houses), these live-in communities were also valued for the commitment-to-each-other fellowship they provided. After all, the yearning for relatedness, as symbolized by Woodstock, was a definite value of the new consciousness — no matter how clumsily, or even perversely, expressed at times. The Jesus people who derived from this same stream found their answer to this yearning in Christian *koinonia*. This took on the "very good" intensity of a completed new creation (see Gen. 1:31 and II Cor. 5:15). And for some, the residential community seemed the best form of this fellowship.

Probably most middle-American Christians had deep reservations about those houses. Many, of course, even questioned the validity of the faith of the Jesus people. But anything communal was particularly suspect, given our cold-war outlook on commun-ism and the fundamentally sexual orientation of our society. Yet, for those who took the time for a closer look, these Christian houses provided a refreshing and impressive contrast to the secular communes. One reporter noted a poster in the living room of a Jesus house: "No drugs, no sex, no hassles: Jesus is Lord!"

This was the grand ideal. But hassles there were nevertheless. Jack Sparks of the Christian World Liberation Front details with open candor, both the joys and the struggles they faced in their early houses and ranch. They thanked God for all that this approach had brought, and continued to mean, to some greatly-changed persons; but the mixture of evangelism, healing of deep problems, and fellowship eventually demanded too much of the permanent residents. It could not go on indefinitely (Sparks 1974:49-102).

Don Williams sees the alumni of the Jesus movement as now somewhat wary about the residential approach to community. A desire for the kind of strong relationships involved is an enduring value of these people; but they are cautious or tentative about joining an intentional community. But then, as we've noted earlier, the new consciousness is characteristically tentative and cautious about all forms of commitment. Nevertheless, some houses have survived and become solid residential communities. Generally, these are the communities where a strong leadership emerged, and they were able to establish a viable economic base (Williams 1975).

The Communitarian Movement

These on-going Christian communities, while valid in themselves, are actually part of a larger stream that is generally referred to as the communitarian movement. While this movement may not be a child of the new consciousness, part (but not all, as we'll see) of it stems from the same source: disenchantment with the technological society and its by-products. Roszak, writing four years after his early counter-culture analysis, sees hope in this movement which he terms, "the visionary commonwealth."

> But there is one way forward: the creation of flesh-and-blood examples of low-consumption, high-quality alternatives to the mainstream pattern of life . . . Communes rural and urban; voluntary primitivism; organic homesteading; extended families . . . Here is the new society piecing itself inventively together within the interstices of the old (1973:387).

> Even if the visionary commonwealth is never more than a relative handful in the city and the wilderness, its role is apt to be like that of the medieval monastics: to exemplify an ideal of life by which the many may judge themselves and the world. The power of such a living example must never be underestimated (ibid:391).

Thank you, Professor Roszak, for a profoundly important application of my chosen historical models to the 1970's.

Not that we need be all that awed by the secular communitarian movement in itself. (Though I do agree with Roszak that it offers some viable alternatives — and examples — to our societal problems.) Our chief interest here is to *understand* our present and emerging *Zeitgeist:* the raw material from which we must structure relevant faith-sharing channels for today and tomorrow. We will certainly not understand this particular phenomenon of our current society if we write off all "communes" as orgiastic centers for hedonists and crackpots. That many communitarians have more idealistic and sober interests, is illustrated by two letters Roszak quotes from *The Mother Earth News:*

> "We have a going project in action now and won't turn down anyone who really wants to live in a spirit-led environment of doing and learning. No drugs, dope or dopes. We have signed contracts for organic produce. Others pick, crate, and truck it; we grow it. We are a co-op, not a commune, and we like yoga and everything organic, try to be Christ-like, and do not believe in killing men or animals . . ."

> "We'd like to start a small village community with private homes for each family and shared labor, costs, food, property, affection and friendship, organic living and growing (we're not vegetarians though), no drugs" (Roszak 1973:393).

Intentional Christian Communities

But we don't have to depend on *The Mother Earth News* for examples. Some of the strongest intentional community models are Christian ones. For example, Reba Place Fellowship in Chicago is nearly twenty years old.

> The impetus to launch this community came from Goshen College in Indiana, which in the forties was taking a new look at the radical reformation in the sixteenth century and the Anabaptist concepts which gave birth to such groups as the Hutterite and Mennonite communities (Jackson 1974:37).

This well-established community is young enough to be part of the present communitarian movement, but experienced enough to be of substantial help to communities just now trying their wings. Reba Place has grown through several stages involving several levels of community style. In the end, they have opted for an essentially total economic community. Their residential arrangements involve a dozen large purchased houses within easy walking distance of each other. Each house contains a "family" of about a dozen people, single and married, including children. Other community members live somewhat more privately in rented apartments nearby.

The probing experiences of this and other groups point to the fact that there is no single "right" way to organize an intentional community. You don't have to live together in a large house and you don't have to share a fully common purse. The community can choose its level of mutual involvement. When that level is agreed on, it is nearly always put in writing (à la the *regulae* of the orders). Whether the families live together or in separate units, they nearly always stress proximity. For community involves not only commitment to one another, but also mutual *support*.

Indeed, one of the purposes of intentional community is to carry the supportive relationships of the small caring, sharing group to a deeper and more permanent level — on a 24-hour basis. This is illustrated in the title of Dave and Neta Jackson's book, *Living Together in a World Falling Apart* — which justifiably lays claim to the status of "A handbook on Christian Community" (1974). This desire for deeper mutual support derives, in part, from an almost-unique feature of American society: the near-total loss of extended family relationships. Compensation for this loss is a conscious motivation of many who join these communities.

That motivation, in itself, provides further evidence of a maturing new consciousness. The disappearance of the extended family in America (and, to a somewhat lesser degree, in other countries of the West) is a relatively recent development, but it has deeply penetrated our culture. We have become an individualistic and privacy-loving people. We build fences (often literally) around our nuclear families. The reversal of these values can hardly be brushed aside as a fad. Furthermore, we are not talking about the early Jesus people houses: temporary havens for teen-agers, newly converted from a state of alienation and purposelessness. We're now looking at communities formed by the well-thought-out choices of fully established adults, many of them with families.

Early in this chapter, I stressed the necessity of a certain order in the three-commitment process of forming a committed community. Most of the examples cited seem to fall short of the third commitment (to task). This partly reflects the current situation, but it has been accentuated by selective reporting on my part. You'll recall that I stressed order of commitment for the purpose of distinguishing the community approach from other valid structures of activism. Then too, this chapter is particularly about community: commitment number two — commitment to one another. In the next two chapters we will move on to the full three-commitment structure.

At the same time, it is important to call attention to the fact that, in a sense, these communities *are* committed to a task (commitment number three). It is not an outward task, but that does not prevent our calling it a task. Now if we name that task "nurture", I am caught in an inconsistency, since throughout this book I have been distinguishing committed communities or sodalities from the nurture structures of the Church. This is why I qualified this paragraph at the outset by citing the inward function of these communities as being a task, "in a sense." And the word "nurture" alone does not adequately describe this present function. We might call it "remedial nurture" since that pin-points the specific or crisis nature of the task.

Many of the relational authors prefer the word "healing". I think I do too. We are only beginning to realize the number of hurting people in our society (and our congregations) — and the depth of their hurts. I'm not talking now about people medically classifiable as disturbed. I'm speaking of inwardly-lonely people, trying to cope with their insecure feelings in a growingly complex society (a "world falling apart") that still tends to glorify an out-grown cultural individualism. Because of this condition of our society, and the paucity of real community in our churches, the healing function of these new caring-community forms is an important — and relevant — task. For Christians who stand in need of such healing, this need must be met before they can validly commit themselves to an outward task.

Admittedly, such communities involve a risk — the risk of turning inward. They are not apt to become as enclosed as some of the harassed radical communities we met in Chapter 4. But many will probably not get beyond nurture. In other words, they will tend to become models of what a congregation should be — a true caring community — rather than the kind of outreaching sodality models we are ultimately looking for. This seems to be the trend at 20-year-old Reba Place. One would hope that at least some of these groups, influenced and informed by the Mennonite heritage, will model themselves on the early Hutterites and the later Moravians who, as we saw, used their community life styles to facilitate their missionary outreach.

What is more likely, realistically, is that the more service-oriented of these groups will center their service on cultural impact and Mennonite distinctives: non-resistance, concern for the oppressed, and similar social issues. This is already happening. Koinonia Partners, an intentional Christian community of Americus, Georgia, "is making possible low-cost housing, employment in rural-based industries, and farm land available on a use basis to Georgia's poor." This community has inspired other groups like Laetare Partners of Rockford, Illinois, which seeks in the same spirit of "a partnership with God and man" to apply these principles in an urban setting (Jackson 1974:295). Personally, I am grateful for the Mennonites' strong Christian witness in these areas which evangelicals have often neglected in recent years. But this emphasis within these communities may also tend to preclude the identification and emergence of cross-cultural gifts in their midst. As a consequence, I suspect, with regret, that these particular communities may fall far short of their historic potential for spinning off missionary sub-communities.

At the same time, it would be erroneous to view the new Christian communitarianism as just a Mennonite phenomenon. As the vanguard, they influence the movement; but others (including some quite separate streams) will influence it as well. Furthermore, some Mennonite groups in America (e.g. the Mennonite Brethren) have been deeply influenced by other evangelical streams; these groups are intensely missionary in addition to their dedication to Mennonite distinctives. In any event, we owe a debt to the young Mennonites who have drawn on their communitarian history and modeled for our period of history the depth of felt-need for supportive relationships within the new consciousness. This is their primary contribution to our present study.

Alternates for Involvement

Nevertheless, before we leave the subject, we should take a look at some of the very practical devices that these communities of sharing have developed (or re-discovered) for coping with a world-falling-apart. Some of these may be directly applicable — even crucial — to the needed new mission models we'll be discussing shortly.

First there is the matter of involvement. As we noted in Chapter 5, nineteenth century Christians felt deeply involved in the new overseas thrusts by giving their money. Some of this feeling still exists in the old consciousness today. But by and large, money-only involvement satisfies fewer and fewer people. We at least need alternates to what we saw Danker referring to as our "collection plate economy" (1971).

More is involved here than simply our attitude toward money. Probably our attitude toward ourselves is the most crucial factor. For we have progressively become a spectator society. The massive growth of professional sports is only a trivial symbol of this. Far more important is the way we have been reduced to on-lookers by those noblemen of our technological society: the expert and the specialist. In the eighteenth century it was the aristocracy; today it is the technocracy. Now, as then, we will release tremendous energy when we again believe that we all have personal worth and can realize worthwhile accomplishments, in groupings of our own choice, without the leave or aid of the professionals or the experts. As we've seen, this was the result of the American Revolution just 200 years ago — the shot heard 'round the world. It can be the genius of a new revolution today without any shot being fired.

Our developing community models are dealing with this problem. In the first place, the "affirmation" of the person and his personal worth is a hallmark of the relational movement. Parallel to this, in Christian communities, is an emphasis on the identification, development and exercise of every member's spiritual gifts. The latter is equally true of the renewed community-like congregations of the body-life movement. These emphases provide a much-needed antidote to the professionalism pervading so many of our institutionalized church structures: a centuries-old problem made more acute by the societal trends.

Now when an intentional community becomes also an economic community and shares a common purse, it can enable the exercise of the gifts of its members to an even fuller extent. Most such communities incorporate a reduced life style as one of their values. The chosen level is usually well short of "poverty"; the emphasis, rather, is on the simple life as discussed in Chapter 6. Yet this avoidance of a consumer orientation, combined with the significant economies of shared facilities (particularly housing and transportation — those two huge items in every family budget), releases a lot of money or labor. It is no longer necessary for everyone to work at a wage-paying job. Members whose gifts are vital, but not marketable, can be set apart by the community to exercise those gifts either part or full time. This is, of course, an extension of the principle by which a congregation supports its pastor. But our tradition-laden handling of this principle has, over the years, become very narrowly defined. The intentional community of consumption can, even in highly-industrialized society, broaden this principle to all applicable gifts.

We can see developing here a combination of personal face-to-face involvement and involvement through money (or the labor that money represents). Admittedly, the dynamics of such an arrangement is stronger in a local situation. Here the mechanically-inclined wage earner (who rejoices in his role), and the community-supported neighborhood evangelist, can frequently share with each other both the joys and the struggles of their respective ministries. We'll hold, for the moment, the application of this to community models of cross-cultural outreach.

Again, intentional communities are cited here only because they effectively *model* some alternatives to money-only involvement. Some of these same principles can be applied short of a totally common purse and a common address. As I've tried to stress throughout this chapter, committed-to-each-other community can be lived out in a variety of styles.

But now we must look for *more* than commitment number two (to each other). This book is ultimately about structures *for mission* – commitment number three, but particularly in the context of cross-cultural missions.

So our next step is to resume our tour of models. What has emerged that young people are drawn to today? Do we see any trends like we saw among Irish youth or among the followers of Francis? If we can pick up any trends, we'll be better prepared for our task in the final chapter: projecting more attractive structures.

CHAPTER 8

Emerging Models

Attractive structures.

I picked up that term in a conversation with Tim, then a young graduate student moving purposefully toward cross-cultural mission involvement. We were talking about those 5000 "card-signers" at Urbana '73 and others like them in discipling groups around the country. Why, I asked, the gap between their strong interest, even commitment, and their action? Why didn't we see more like himself, preparing and going?

Obviously Tim had already given this a lot of thought. He came right back with two answers, one of which was: lack of attractive structures.

Tim's other reply is not so easily reduced to just a few words. It centers around our attempts to communicate the missionary task to these young people. We tend to major on "challenge", but they want information (my translation). Because they don't really understand what's involved, they're wary about committing themselves to the task. I've checked this evaluation out with others who, like Tim, have broken through and are on their way. They confirm that our mission education isn't adequately coming through to their peers — even in our strongest mission-minded churches. In fact, they say our communication is geared to the middle-age supporters. Our mission-oriented congregations need to consider this feedback. But at best they are handicapped. For, as we saw in Chapter 6, the people of the new consciousness need more than words when it somes to really vital communications; and they have understandable reasons (however subconscious) for going slow on longer range career commitments.

These factors lie behind the "short term" concept of missionary recruitment that has become such a fact of life within the past decade. This kind of communication by toe-in-the-water experimental involvement has served to supplement our apparently inadequate verbal communication. The concept is now widely accepted within the missionary establishment, and has opened a channel for at least a segment of today's young adults to get involved.

Appealing to other segments are a number of structures that we might call youth sodalities. These groups tend to combine the involvement-communication of short term experiences with some further youth-attractive characteristics. And as we'll see in a moment, just as we saw in our historical tour, "attractive" in this context does not mean fun and games!

But first I want to introduce my sketches of these models with a recognition that they are only that: sketches. All of them deserve at least chapter-long treatment, and some warrant full-thesis research. I hope some grad students will pick up that challenge. But it will serve our immediate purpose to confine ourselves to this brief survey.

Operation Mobilization

In 1961, a group of 25 students drew up a "manifesto of world evangelism" in which they committed themselves to a revolutionary life style. Here are some excerpts:

> And we *are* revolutionaries! We are only a small group of Christian young people in Operation Mobilization, yet we have determined by God's grace to live our lives according to the revolutionary teachings of our Master . . . This is our commitment, and we will press forward until every person has heard the gospel . . . The world is our goal! And our primary targets are the seemingly impenetrable areas of the Communist and Moslem countries which can only receive freedom as they have opportunity to receive the Truth. These countries will be reached for Christ no matter what the cost. The ultimate victory is ours! (Verwer 1972:13-16).

To be sure, "revolutionary" was a popular term in the rhetoric of the

60's. But here is a group that has lived out its high demand for commitment over a 15 year period and shows no signs of blunting the edge of that expectancy. The manifesto from which I've quoted appears as the first chapter of founder George Verwer's book entitled, significantly, *Come! Live! Die!*

This is clearly a missionary sodality with a strong "commitment number three." But the *primary* focus of the group, just as clearly, is commitment number one: to the Lord. The short-term summer programs, involving one to two thousand young people, are geared to on-the-job training in discipleship. Personal growth, spiritual reality and stronger commitment are stressed. The simple life, forsaking all for Christ, and zeal for service are values the group seeks to inculcate in its participant-trainees.

We see here some obvious echoes from our historic models: a certain monastic-like starkness and austerity relative to the current values of Western society. In fact, the OM life-style may be just a bit too demanding for most American youth. For despite its American origins, OM today draws most of its summer participants from Europe, the Near East and beyond. Only 10% of the 1500 who normally participate are apt to come from the States — another 50-75 from Canada. In part, this stems from a purposely lower profile recruitment effort in America. In any case, the fact remains that a significant number of Western young people, drawn from relatively traditional sources (Bible schools and established campus groups), seem to find OM more attractive than other, less-austere options. Apparently George Verwer understands the attractiveness of this demanding "Christian reality" he preaches. For he originally wanted his publisher to call his book, "Hunger for Reality." This is a penetrating insight into the new consciousness.

We see another echo from the past in the direct missionary strategy of OM. As a team of perhaps 40 young people moves into a European town for a summer month, all their energies are directed toward working with all local churches that desire their help. While they perceive themselves as on the front lines of evangelism, they do nothing toward planting a new church in their own name. They work only with existing churches (and/or missionaries where applicable). But like some of the monastic revivals we viewed earlier, the not-so-hidden objective is the *renewal* of the churches they are assisting.

Typically, 350 summer participants will ask to stay on for a one or two year assignment — sometimes with an open-ended possibility for a longer commitment. These attend a month-long training camp somewhere in Europe. OM avoids investment, so they hold this in whatever facilities the Lord provides. It might be a warehouse they're given the use of in return for cleaning it up a bit. Sleeping bags are a must. All the permanent field leaders are present for this month, counselling with those who are interested in their respective fields.

While OM has no conscious emphasis on the kind of community dynamics we've been discussing, at this late summer training camp community-like teams do form. The young people have, of course, already experienced supportive relationships in the previous month of evangelistic work. Now they can build on this as they plan for a bit longer period of service together. Though commitment number two (to each other) is not intentionally built into the model, the nature of OM as a youth sodality, made up primarily of more or less new consciousness people, breeds communities almost automatically.

Structurally, OM is determined to maintain a low profile. Theoretically at least, even the "permanent" staff — including Verwer himself — make a fresh decision annually as to whether they will continue. Summer participant-trainees are told that they are neither joining nor working for an organization; "you *are* the movement!" While no movement can resist completely the inevitable trend toward institutionalization, OM seems to have done very well in its effort to impede this process.

Youth With A Mission

This youth sodality is clearly in the same genre with OM. They came into being about the same time and under somewhat similar circumstances; they both deal substantially with short-term participant-trainees. But there are also interesting diversities that provide young people a choice. For example, YWAM also believes in the simple life, but projects a less austere image. One might say it reflects more of a joy-image, like the early Franciscans. (But, I must immediately add: this does not suggest that OM is joyless!) Perhaps the Pentecostal-charismatic background of its original leadership partly influences this.

YWAM also makes a conscious effort to keep the

now-world-wide movement from being overly American. And the leadership is very consciously wrestling with structural questions — not, as so often happens, with a focus on "controlling" the mushrooming movement; but rather in search of ways to preserve the movement's dynamics. As one leader put it, they were once primarily traveling bands; now they are more like migrating communities that are beginning to put some roots down. This group is more consciously aware of its community dimensions, and is busily studying the Anabaptist and Pietist models. Body-life principles are also in evidence. Community to community links involve leader (or elder) relationships that are more horizontal than pyramidical. This gives YWAM somewhat of an "umbrella" relationship to its more developed sub-communities. We'll be taking a more detailed look at one of these communities later in this chapter.

In its short-term dimension, YWAM also attracts large numbers of young people. It draws from a somewhat different segment than OM, although the streams are not that far apart. It has an even less traditional image and draws from less traditional sources. Those we once called flower children would probably incline toward YWAM. Many are alumni of the Jesus movement. Many come from Pentecostal churches, charismatic groups and less structured fellowships. I indicated above that they tend to be successors to the young friends of Francis. Interestingly, that identification was made more pointed at a Christian Fair held at the Orange County Fairgrounds here in Southern California in the summer of 1974. YWAM sponsored one building where its films were shown, including one that pictured their substantial effort to reach people for Christ at the Munich Olympic games. These showings were well attended. But YWAM had also rented a copy of "Brother Son, Sister Moon" — Hollywood's rather perceptive portrayal of Francis. They showed this periodically through the week-end, and each showing was packed out with young people.

Those young people who are attracted to YWAM have a variety of training-involvement options. For example, in addition to the summer programs, there are schools of evangelism in Europe of 9 months duration. Here, too, there is the emphasis on personal growth and discipleship that had led me to refer to the short-termers of both groups as participant-trainees. This term also points to the fact that such training becomes a potential door to further service. While for some this means further involvement with the same group, neither OM nor YWAM is interested in absorbing all of this potential. They *want* their alumni to spread out in many avenues of service; they welcome competition. Research is needed to see if this potential is being realized. Or are we losing this potential because we lack the attractive structures?

While OM and YWAM represent the "big two" of the new youth *missionary* sodalities, they are not alone in this field. For the youth sodalities that have been prominent on U.S. college campuses since World War II are increasingly involved in overseas outreach themselves. Let's look briefly at how the "big three" of these campus groups fit into the overall picture today.

Campus Sodalities

The Navigators had a cross-cultural missionary dimension even before their Stateside center of gravity moved from military personnel to the U.S. campus scene. Inter-Varsity Christian Fellowship has long had an overseas outreach through the related International Fellowship of Evangelical Students. The younger Campus Crusade for Christ has more recently adopted a strong global emphasis via its World Thrust program, and, more directly, its Agape program involving short-term (two year) overseas experiences.

The Agape program is too young to have a reportable track record. But I have every reason to believe that this will prove itself to be another youth-attractive structure. It will probably fall roughly into the same category as OM and YWAM, but draw from still another segment of the youth culture. Like YWAM, it projects a joy-image. But it will probably draw students who either appreciate the more highly organized character of the parent structure — or who at least have no quarrel with this business management image. I foresee Agape attracting these young people in large numbers. Though many of these may find more permanent service in other international aspects of the Crusade program, there should be plenty of potential left over to feed other missionary efforts.

The Navigators have a different kind of highly-organized image — something of a military bearing deriving from the group's origins.

But as we've noted earlier, something interesting happened on the way to the 1970's. While many authority *symbols* (most notably the military and the police) were rejected by the counter culture, the clearer-eyed among them did not throw out the baby with the bath water; they did not reject authority as such. Some, in fact, tend to major on authority, and even discipline. Hence the attraction of monastic-like groups such as OM. And thus the Navigators' stress on discipline is suddenly very up-to-date. Then too, the group itself has by no means been standing still. Whereas it once reflected the cultural trend of American evangelicalism to exalt standing alone for Christ, there is an added emphasis today on supportive relationships which, as we've seen, lays the foundation for community dynamics.

Don't look for mushroom-like "movement" growth in the Navigators; they are too heavily committed to painstaking one-to-one discipling. However, when you've been at the one-to-one approach as long and as determinedly as the Navigators have, there are a lot of old "ones" for the new "ones" to relate to! Hence this structure of high commitment demand may both attract and absorb fairly large numbers in the years just ahead.

It is hard to compare IVCF to the other groups since the countable paid staff plays an intentionally background-consultative role in this student-led movement. The same is true of the IFES staff. This tends to preclude the possibility of the latter absorbing very many of the alumni of the former even if such service should prove increasingly attractive to the serious students who form the core of this movement. Inter-Varsity will probably continue to feed other missionary movements. In the United Kingdom, this is a major source of OM participants. And in North America, the triennial "Urbana" has, in the past two decades, played a significant role in recruitment for the whole missionary movement.

We have referred several times to how the '73 Urbana also became a barometer signaling an upsurge of interest in cross-cultural missionary service. And the yet-to-be-answered questions revolve around how, where, and by whom this increased potential will be channeled into positive activity. So far, we've been speaking of short-term service as the intermediate step between strong interest and longer-range involvement — a learning experience on which to base an intelligent commitment. Following Urbana '73 another option developed to serve this function: the Summer Institute of International Studies.

This effort, hurriedly designed in the spring of 1974 soon after the "card signing" results of Urbana were known, has been backed by a wide spectrum of evangelical missions professors and missionary leaders. I've been privileged to have a part-time staff leadership role myself. We designed this learning program to fill the information-for-commitment gap we've been speaking of — something beyond that which is possible in a 5-day exposure, even such an excellently-executed one as Urbana. Because the SIIS program carries transferable academic credit, more students can afford to participate including many who lack the resources or backing to take part in an overseas involvement program. Yet this is clearly pre-vocational training, and direct recruitment is avoided; students are challenged to world consciousness regardless of where in that world they serve. The program has attracted both undergraduate and graduate students — even career young people. Most come from secular campuses.

SIIS enrollment the first two summers has been relatively small: between 40 and 60 students per term. As a result, the sharing of information by highly-regarded missions professors could be carried out in a relatively informal manner. And because these professors lived in the dorm with the students, a learning community developed that proved life-changing for many of the participants. Some of the alumni are currently pursuing vocational training as a community for later involvement in the Muslim world.

Turning now from the on-campus spectrum, we should note at least one youth sodality model that is closer to the dynamics of that once-more-visible part of the new consciousness we commonly refer to as alienated or counter-cultural.

Dilaram Ministries

The first Dilaram House, which so impressed me during my visit to Kabul, Afghanistan, has now expanded into Dilaram Ministries with a base and training facilities in Amsterdam (where the "world travelers" usually set out on the "trail" across Asia), and several houses in key cities along the trail. New houses are developing in other places as well. This is a truly new consciousness structure: former street people ministering to people who are still a part of that scene (which continues to be quite visible in Europe). The houses are residential communities geared to evangelism and initial growth. The impressive young leader of this ministry, Floyd McClung, earlier did a short term of service with YWAM, but founded the Kabul house separately. Now he has placed this work under the developing YWAM umbrella, less for the service facilities involved than for the mutually supportive spiritual relationships between elders and leaders of the YWAM components.

Dilaram is not yet a cross-cultural ministry, strictly speaking, even though many nationalities (mostly European and North American) are involved. It works within the youth sub-culture which, in many ways, is more homogeneous than some countries today. At the same time, many of these young people have either traveled the trail, or will in the future be serving at some point in North Africa or Asia. They are getting a good deal of cross-cultural exposure. Downtrack, this may prove to be a launching pad for cross-cultural involvement. As I indicated in the Introduction, I hope to find emerging within such groups a reasonable number of people with cross-cultural gifts. As I note their detachment regarding personal possessions, I hear echoes of some of the missionary pioneers of the past century. When I note their interest in crafts and other physically creative tasks, I see potential new links with Third World people.

For the purpose of our study, the Dilaram model is most interesting because it is fully a part of the current Christian communitarian movement (strong commitment number two — to each other), yet uses this as a vehicle for *evangelistic* outreach. Lately, this group, too, has been studying the Anabaptist and Moravian models; and it is interested in the social perspectives of the Mennonite-influenced "young evangelicals." But it also sits at the feet of men like Francis Schaeffer and F.F. Bruce. It seems to have the cultural and evangelistic mandates — along with healing ("remedial nurture") and discipleship training — all in good balance.

Dilaram not only is a community, but perceives itself as having a mission to share its community perspectives. To this end it has recently designed and offered short term involvement-training in community-based ministry potential. This is clearly a model to watch.

The Tonga Team

This model stands somewhat between the youth missionary sodalities we've been examining and traditional mission efforts. We should note here that even though the Protestant missionary movement gave birth to the voluntary society model, this structure has not been an exclusive vehicle of the movement. Thousands of missionaries have been sent out by "free church" groups that eschew "organization" on theological grounds. The local congregation or assembly is the only recognized structural form. The two most notable examples with a strong missionary thrust are the Cambellian tradition (Christian Churches and Churches of Christ) and the so-called Plymouth Brethren. As we've noted earlier, there is no such thing as non-structure. So the far-ranging missionaries of these organization-rejecting traditions do have a structured relationship to their sending congregations, and each other, no matter how low the profile of that structure may be.

But when Phil Elkins and several fellow students from Churches of Christ background met during their missionary training, a team spirit developed which had at least the kind of structure experienced by those young seminarians of the haystack prayer meeting. A commitment to one another developed. As they thought about overseas service, the four couples and one single fellow involved found a growing attraction to the idea of serving together — as a team. As they projected this idea into the "structure" of their tradition, they recognized that the links of supportive relationships between a local congregation and its missionaries was a key element of the barely-visible infra-structure of the movement. So even though they were all from different congregations that might have supported them, they sought out a local church that would be willing to send and support the whole team, enhancing their unity.

They found a not-very-large congregation, with a much larger faith, that made a five-year commitment to them. As a next step, they identified by research a place where such a team could make a particularly valuable contribution: a part of the Tonga tribe (Zambia) that had minimal exposure to the Gospel.

In carrying out their ministry there, the team-ness of their effort proved particularly rewarding in enabling each one to pursue his gift and interest. The resulting role specialization they practiced seems, again, to stand mid-way between the skills orientation of so many mission structures today and the spiritual gifts emphasis of new consciousness Christian communities. The dynamics of this team was not self-consciously "relational"; the members come from a more traditional stream. This illustrates again the wide variety of application of our thesis. At the same time, it was clear to me in talking to Phil Elkins that the relationships established in the joint training period yielded above-average mutual support in the field situation.

Bethany Fellowship

This model doesn't quite fit our chapter title. It can hardly be said that Bethany Fellowship is "emerging". It emerged way back in 1945. But our tour of current models would be quite incomplete without it. For it not only "anticipated" the current Christian communitarian movement; it also serves as an interesting precursor of the *missionary* community models that this book is all about.

Bethany began as a Pietist-model conventicle (Chapter 4) within a Lutheran congregation, but the inevitable tension resulted in the formation of a separate community. The first member families pursued a course of Bible study that grew into a Bible school. This led to an early involvement in publishing which is still growing, as evidenced by Bethany's advertisements in Christian periodicals.

Bethany is an economic community in the Hutterite and Moravian sense of developing its own industries. Besides publishing, the community manufactures Bethany Trailers, a patio grill and other products. The Minneapolis complex includes several apartment units where the "here" members of this on-purpose missionary community reside. "There" sub-communities carry on missionary work in the West Indies, Brazil, Indonesia and the Philippines. These communities follow the home community pattern of combining a Bible school with a publishing arm. The "here" Minneapolis community has a supportive relationship to the "there" thrusts.

From the perspective of our study, Bethany was not only ahead of its time, but appears to have been "born out of due season." For

1945 America, in hindsight, was not exactly a "community" era! On the other hand, we've been seeing throughout this study that the committed community model has a broad range of applications — today as well as throughout history. So it should not really surprise us that the founders of Bethany chose this structural form long before there was any visible "new consciousness". For we are not, after all, saying that missionary communities are valid only for the new consciousness; rather, it is the fact of that consciousness which makes the wider application of community structures for mission so imperative and urgent.

We started this chapter talking about "attractive" structures — and better means of communicating an understanding of missions. For I agree with my friend, Tim, that these are two key factors in the gap between interest and participation. But then Tim made one more observation about his seemingly-reluctant friends:

"They won't go alone!"

That sums up a great deal of what we've been pointing toward in this book. And we must now come to terms with the practical ramifications of this as we further think through the new and revised mission models we need for today and tomorrow.

CHAPTER 9

Creating Committed Communities

Marriage is the smallest and most intense form of committed community. Marriages can be "created" in a variety of ways. For most of history, and even for most of the world's peoples today, marriages have been "arranged" — that is, by others. I don't find very many Americans, of *any* consciousness, about to salute this custom! Yet, as we've seen, this is virtually the only way our present mission sodalities create those sub-teams that do exist in their midst.

Recently, I had a ring-side seat for a courtship that developed within an intentional Christian community. The young man, in good Western tradition, took the initiative in letting his interest be known. Then the community lovingly joined with the couple in seeking God's will. This involved both prayer and counsel — but counsel "with" rather than counsel "to". When the couple made their decision, this was "confirmed" by the community.

I believe we have a similar "mix" of personal and community choice/guidance in the creation of the first missionary band (Acts 13:2). That verse contains at least an implication that the Holy Spirit had spoken to Barnabas and Saul before he asked the leadership team they were a part of to confirm that call by releasing them for other service. This is probably the "ideal" for forming a new community — be it a new family (marriage) or a new missionary team.

I also consider it "ideal" that committed communities arise out of the life of a local congregation. Under present conditions, this will probably happen only in those congregations with a body-life emphasis that have, in turn, attracted significant numbers of college and post-college young people. For the mutual caring — and trusting — relationships of a true community are clear pre-requisites for the mutual guidance examples we've cited above. We noted in Chapter 1 that this sense of community is in poor repair in our society, and in most of our congregations. Consequently, young people of the new consciousness who have found Christ, or a deepened personal faith, outside the structured congregations have tended to make very tenuous entry or re-entry into these congregations — if at all.

Forming Communities

Consequently, we need practical alternatives for both of these "ideals". In the first instance, we see that committed people must make responsible *personal* choices in forming a true community, regardless of the availability of confirmation by others. So it was for the early monks — and for Francis and his friends. In this case, confirmation comes from the mutual guidance and resultant commitment to one another (which will most often be a process rather than an event). I will not go so far as to say that this matter of personal, mutual choice of teammates is pre-requisite to community. But I am convinced that it is crucial for American Christians at this point in history. Arranged marriages can work satisfactorily in other cultures. And we saw in Chapter 5 that in our existing missionary sodalities, "assigned" teams just may develop community. But our whole purpose here is to do our very best to *build this into* a truly relevant model for today.

In the second instance, a committed community can't very well form unless committed people have some place to find each other. The principal alternates to the local congregation, of course, are Christian colleges and the campus sodalities. This has been true for Christian marriage for many years. However, with present trends to extended schooling and delayed career choices, such community formation is more apt to take place during graduate training. That means we need further alternates for those now out of college — and those who have chosen post high school education outside the formal school structures. We've seen the team and community forming potential of groups like OM and YWAM. The many discipling groups across the country also have great potential — if they can catch a vision of the world. Some alumni of the Summer Institute of International Studies are seeking to develop a Fellowship of World Christians which is more a movement than a structure at present. They seek to enhance world consciousness within the campus sodalities, discipling groups and other frameworks where people of growing commitment may meet each other.

I trust that none of what I've said above will lead committed young Christians to believe they can justifiably ignore, write-off, or be quite independent of the established structures of the Church: either its congregations or its sodalities. We'll be discussing interstructural relationships shortly. Right now we are talking only about the formative process. And if our historical survey revealed anything, it demonstrated that creative new vehicles of commitment seldom originate with the establishment — particularly in times of great change. Papa simply does not always know best. Besides certain disadvantages he has in discerning the winds of change, he inevitably gets trapped in conserving and peace-keeping roles. As we've seen, creative new energy usually generates from the committed young. I want today's responsible young Christians to feel comfortable about taking such initiative, recognizing that this is not only valid, but actually crucial to this period of history in which they live and are called to serve. Relationships with other structures of the Body can — and must — follow later.

But while autonomous (something quite different than "independent") initiative is valid here, a self-selecting community had better be based on more than good vibes, as they say. Just as a marriage had better be based on more than chemistry. Good vibes may validly open the kind of dialogue that could lead to community. But responsible, committed young Christians will look for more than this as their relationship-toward-community develops and grows. I know they will. I've watched them seek this growth prior to making final decisions about marriage.

Developing Community

One factor is particularly vital in this growth process. Or perhaps we should be speaking of a testing or confirming process, analogous to pre-engagement serious dating. One crucial goal of Christian community is body life. I've maintained that the sodality has a biblical right to a life of its own — that it is not a dependent or para-structure to the congregational/linkage structure of the Church. However, if the sodality fails to develop a body life of its own, the clerical trend to assign it subsidiary status has some point. But, of course, this need not be the case. The first step is confirmation that *complementary gifts* are present to the point where the community can function as a body. To adapt Paul's language of I Corinthians 12, if the people that feel drawn together are all "arms", you might have some kind of fellowship but you certainly won't have a body. A "whole" body is vital to the kind of sodality we're seeking. And "checking" for a complementary balance of gifts is particularly necessary in the relatively small communities I visualize. So the identification of these gifts is of primary importance in the confirmation process.

Once you are sure you have a body — not a truncated torso — that body needs some time to function as such in relatively congenial surroundings. It needs some modest track record before heading for the Olympics. Deuteronomy 24:5 prescribes this for marriage: "When a man is newly married, he shall not go out with the army or be charged with any business; he shall be free at home one year, to be happy with his wife whom he has taken." Boy, has that one ever fallen through the cracks in our industrialized society! It's interesting to note that some intentional communities are restoring this sensible Old Testament principle. As we've seen, a community of consumption has that kind of flexibility.

In the case of an intentional missionary community, the ideal situation for this kind of body-life growth is a time of learning centered on cross-cultural studies. Besides preparing the community for years of ministry together, this approach has a unique double-edged value in preparing for that bogeyman of all new missionaries: culture shock. The cross-cultural studies give the coping *skills;* and an already-developed community life provides the caring *support.* What a combination!

I would suggest that a developing missionary community carefully consider its residential arrangements during this group learning experience. The one-large-house-extended-family approach is too intense for me, but not for many of today's young adults. Even those who would not salute this approach long range may find it not only acceptable but attractive for the initial community-building period. If not, I would certainly recommend that the separate residences at least be as proximate as possible. Economic arrangements should also be considered in terms of their training value. This might involve a different level than the planned longer-range standards. As we've noted throughout this study, there is no one "right" arrangement for everyone. But sharing, as a principle, must be operative in some very tangible manner. And as we've also noted in all our models, once standards are agreed on, they should be written down — not as "laws", but like those standards-for-reference that are kept at the Bureau of Standards.

Residential arrangements have to be considered all over again when the community finds its field of service. What's good for the community has to fit in with what is best for the task. Even an easy-walking-distance proximity might not be feasible; the members might have to scatter themselves in a city or district to be effective witnesses. But they ought to remain close enough geographically to meet frequently; they need to maintain their supportive commitment to each other. The *quality* of the community is the essential ingredient, not the form. Nevertheless, the community must evaluate periodically whether the form is adequate to maintain the quality.

Relating to the Body

While the reality of body life in any structured community of the Church (whether a congregation or a sodality) validates its autonomy, it can not warrant its independence! For the Body life of the larger Body of Christ also depends on the exercise of the gifts of its "members". This biological analogy need not, in this case, be limited to the host of individual believers that make up the Body, but can justifiably be applied to its many communities as well. And it is a rare community of the Church that does not have significant relational ties with other communities — even within traditions that are dogmatically congregational. Surely the new committed missionary communities will want such relationships.

In the next few pages, I want to suggest three models for such relationships. These models certainly do not exhaust the possibilities. In fact, this whole chapter is designedly non-comprehensive; I am far more interested in stimulating thinking and discussion than I am in "answers". The relationships I'm suggesting may exist from the very founding of the new community — as in the "ideal" case of the very first Barnabas/Saul missionary band. Or, for reasons we've discussed, these relationships may have to wait a bit. Our historical overview of the long delays in solving tensions between emerging sodalities and established churchly structures should prompt us to patience.

A Community-Within-Mission Model

I want to explore first the possibility of relating some of these small community teams to existing mission sodalities. I want to do this both positively and realistically. For I believe both are implied in Jesus' allusion to wine and wineskins (Matt. 9:17). Nothing is said about tossing out the old wineskins. In fact, the opposite objective is clearly stated: ". . . so both are preserved." New "movement" wine can be corrosive on institutionalized wineskins. The new wave of missionary energy that I believe is trying to break surface might well "break" asunder some of our present skins. And, as I've personally observed, the new consciousness wine can be particularly irritating to the throats of missionaries who live much of their lives in relative isolation from it — then are periodically plopped into "future shock."

Yet, as we've seen, the new consciousness is not a type but a spectrum. *Some* of the communities we're discussing may fit in *some* of our existing sodalities. At best this involves some risk, but realistic planning can reduce that risk. Mission leaders rightly feel strong responsibility to their existing members, and must consider new approaches in the light of their potential effect on these people. On the basis of personal experience with overseeing planned organizational change, I'd suggest two basic steps in receiving group applications from these new communities.

First, look on this as a new approach calling for a separate division of the mission. In a slightly different context, the Cornelius Corps of the Greater Europe Mission is a model for this (which needs analysis once it has developed a track record). You might even want to think of it as an experimental or research project. This relates to my second suggestion: look for a new field for the already-in-community people, preferably a good distance from existing fields.

On the other side of the coin, the mission will have to recognize that it is dealing with a whole new set of dynamics. This will begin with the application-selection process. A group application will have to involve something more (and less) than looking at that many individual applications. The tone set by the consideration of the group application may enhance or jeopardize the experiment.

Needless to say, the "senior missionary" idea does not fit the model — with one exception. Any mission that would even consider these suggestions, will have a few experienced people who are trying to understand — and, more importantly, appreciate many dimensions of — the new consciousness. The young people gravitate to such people, and vice versa. Ask one such couple to help the young community get established in their new surroundings. This can be a very temporary service function. Yet if you choose well, the young people may not let them go. But don't make the mistake of then assuming that this experienced man is the leader — reporting to the "home office." That's a rather sure way to lose the ball game. In fact, it takes the game right back to the old playing field. Leadership will have emerged within the group long before departure. (But remember, it doesn't look like our models.) The experienced couple, if they are urged to stay and join the community, will probably get slotted into an ideal role of highly-respected counselors where they have all the influential advantages of leadership without the administrative and other disadvantages.

Let's suppose that such an experiment proves highly successful in ABC Mission. Within five years, several thriving community teams overshadow the original form of the mission. And let's suppose that instead of this threatening the older members, they themselves form communities in each field with a strong sense of commitment to each other. What then happens to the management model of the original sodality? It could become a new "umbrella" model with two foci: servicing the communities' practical needs; and a framework for mutually supportive leader/elder relationships between communities. We've seen this model emerging in a younger sodality, Youth With A Mission.

None of this will happen easily. And resistance may come less from individual preferences than from the drag built into organizational machinery. The staff leadership may want to move, but the more conservative board members may have their doubts. And these, in turn, may well cite the conservative constituency as their reason. This is not just a matter of passing the buck. Mission board members are, in fact, trustees; they hold assets in trust. But in trust for whom? For the Lord? For the sodality membership? Or for the supporting constituency? After many decades in which the management model has increasingly pervaded these structures, the constituency is often viewed as the "stockholders" — not legally but emotionally. As with stockholders, the constituency looks to the board (which, in turn, looks to the administration) to *control*. And the means of control is money. This may represent the largest practical problem in trying to put the new wine into the old wineskins. The potential for rupture is considerable.

In the light of this "realism" (which some might view as negativism), why do I suggest this model at all — even on such a selective basis. Principally because, if carefully and selectively handled, it carries potential for some renewal of our existing structures. In the end, people and their movements — even their institutions — are *more* than wine and wineskins. That was only meant to be a parabolic figure. In the reality of live people and actual movements, our proper goal is not just the preservation of both old and new, but that both may abound!

Mission leaders may be attracted to this model because of its potential for avoiding what they like to call "proliferation". This word, I feel, has suffered a fate similar to "radical" as discussed in Chapter 5. Mission leaders and pastors just seem to assume it is wrong. Why? Was it wrong when your mission was founded? Presumably at that juncture of history there was room for *one* more mission. Or perhaps your mission resulted from an unnecessary personality conflict; "But the Lord has blessed its ministry despite this." Sounds like Barnabas' Cyprus team! Can't you just hear one of those nit-picking Hebrew believers down in Jerusalem groaning about the "proliferation of those missionary bands out of Antioch" when that happened? We simply must face up to the arrogance involved in assuming we know how many sodality structures the Holy Spirit plans to use.

Still, I recognize that there are some very practical problems in the proliferation of *organizations* — with all that implies in American practice. Duplicate administrative machinery can be expensive. At the same time, the supposed efficiency of larger administrative units can be elusive. For administrative staffs proliferate too – *within* an organization. And once you pass the minimal-paid-staff level, administration is seldom as efficient again. Administrative chores feed on the administrative staff as they do on the rest of the staff. It is a dog-chasing-tail proposition, office equipment and computers notwithstanding. Of course, a service-only "administration" can be kept much leaner than one involving management/control. So the "umbrella" model may be one solution. However, some of the small well-knit communities I envision may have minimum servicing needs. They may learn to reduce house-keeping chores to a level where a service unit is helpful but not crucial.

And this lower-profile trend may also help reduce "proliferation" tension in another area: the dunning PR that now deluges congregations and individual Christians. Here I can sympathize with the pastors of mission-hearted churches who often are the leading critics of proliferation. For they simply cannot maintain meaningful relationships with so many structures. In a moment, I would like to offer these pastors a possible solution — *with* proliferation! Not organizational proliferation, to be sure. But sodality proliferation: small committed communities overseas, each vitally related to a congregation at home, whether through a mission service structure (as per our model above) or not. With nearly three billion people yet to be reached for Christ, we certainly need some proliferation of the congregational structure of the Church! (Let's now call this "multiplication"; we still view that word positively.) And if we can properly adjust our sights, our strategies, our models and our relationships, we need at least some multiplication of the sodality structure: the New Testament means of planting those new congregations.

A Congregation/Community Model

We've already met a prototype of this model in the last chapter. The Tonga Team had a here/there relationship with a single congregation that was highly beneficial to both communities — like other here/there relationships we've noted in our historical survey.

We noted that the Tonga Team was related to one of the thousands of congregations that have always sent their missionaries out directly, without the agency of an organized society. Most of those congregations have followed the same cultural trends as the missions; that is, they send individuals and couples rather than teams. But this is easily adapted. Even in the case of smaller congregations, several in near proximity can combine to share in the support of a there-community. And, of course, this model is adaptable to a wider circle of congregations than those who have traditionally worked this way.

As we apply this model to the small new missionary communities we're visualizing, we'll probably find them relating best to those congregations that are, themselves, experiencing significant growth of community consciousness through one of several renewal movements: relational caring/sharing groups; body life, with its emphasis on the spiritual gifts of all members; and the charismatic renewal. Such an understanding and appreciation of community provides an ideal foundation for a full-orbed here/there *community* relationship.

Out of such renewed congregations, there-communities may actually originate. But even if the two find each other later, I hope they will take the time to develop caring and trusting relationships between the two communities. Out of this can grow a commitment to each other on a group-to-group level. The Tonga Team developed a relatedness to its supporting congregation during its period of cross-cultural studies together. Since I am advocating that this is a good time for the prospective there-community to develop its own internal dynamics, that might be a bit much to try to accomplish all at once. But not necessarily.

At any rate, the quality of the here/there relationship must not only be established; it must be cultivated and maintained over the years. If trusting relationships break down, the congregation may slip into a variation of this here/there model which we must be careful to avoid.

We noted in Chapter 5 how early nineteenth century Christians revelled in their new opportunities to be involved in Christian action (including missionary outreach) via their money. This money-as-involvement aspect of legal tender is still very fulfilling to many Christians, though they are fewer in number as we've noted.

Meanwhile, our society has come to accentuate another aspect of money: money-as-power, or control. This is by no means new; it's merely more virulent today. And while we strongly object to this at the national political level since Watergate, we are more accepting of it than we realize at the business management level — on which I believe we have unwarily patterned some of our intra and inter-structural relationships in the Church. This was implied in our Chapter 5 discussion about the internal management of our voluntary societies. Here I'm more concerned about congregation/sodality tensions, which very much involve money — and control.

I became more fully aware of the extent of these tensions when I joined the official board of the Interdenominational Foreign Mission Association in 1970. These tensions surfaced more visibly at the Green Lake Consultation in the fall of 1971. At that time, I found myself rather sympathetic with the pastors who were a bit weary of their congregations being looked on as money machines for the missions. They were right in wanting more of a partnership (which the model we're presently discussing provides). Yet the pastors who have been most vocal about this have not necessarily provided an attractive alternative, in my view. Under the rubric of "responsibility", I see money-by-control pressures building up that are downright carnal. Brethren, these things ought not to be.

It is for this reason that I do not recommend the congregation/community model to just any congregation that can financially afford it. Unless the here/there linkage is based strongly on authentic trusting relationships (in which money becomes quite incidental), the model will probably fail. But renewed congregations capable of the requisite trusting relationships are multiplying. It is my prayer that these congregations and multiplying committed communities centered on cross-cultural missions will find each other.

A Community/Community Model

This model is a variation of the one above; only the "here" community is one of the new intentional communities rather than a traditional congregation. As indicated in Chapter 7, I suspect, with regret, that relatively few of these communities will take on a world perspective. But I have hope that some will. And when this happens, the way they approach structural linkage between the here-community and the spin-off there-community will be instructive for all of us. For here the new consciousness will be most fully at work. That's not to say they won't blunder. But they will also produce creative designs.

Here I would like to speculate on some of the elements that might appear as this model develops.

First, I doubt that an intentional community would start from the presupposition that it had to fully support, with money, this new sub-community. The "here" group would probably be willing to stand as guarantor, as required, for visa and other purposes. And they might want to have the privilege of some money-sharing. But given the usual outlook on community involvement, they might well urge the researching fore-runners of the planned missionary sub-community to seek out jobs for some of their members, as a means of becoming more integrally a part of the villages or neighborhoods where they would live and witness. This is a tough assignment. Developing countries of the Third World are protecting, for their own people, more and more of the positions in which westerners used to be welcome. The researchers would have to be creative and optimistic people!

They would be helped in this by a second difference in pre-suppositions: life style. We seldom stop to consider the degree to which we limit our options by our presumption of what constitutes a minimum life style. I'm not suggesting that new consciousness communitarians will be unfettered in this matter. But they do start from different givens. Therefore more (but not unlimited) options are open to them. In the present case, they wouldn't be limited to jobs paying near-western salaries.

Finally, I see these people as probably more open to changing their citizenship — an option which may open considerable opportunities, once we can start thinking about this in terms of today. So often when this subject is discussed within existing mission circles, we only review yesterday's negative conclusions which were based on a very different kind of world — and a different consciousness. For example, we lay great stress on our children. New consciousness people are no less devoted to their children; but that does not pre-suppose American education. I have expectations anyway that the new consciousness may some day be able to pull us out of the school-room boxes we've nailed ourselves into — and some committed missionary communities, patterned on the above model, may provide the fertile soil in which creative new approaches to *learning* can be incubated.

Other Options

This attempt to visualize what a spin-off missionary sub-community of the Christian communitarian movement might look like, bears some resemblance to a style of missions proposed by John Howard Yoder 15 years ago — before the new consciousness and the current communitarian movement were visible. He called it "migration evangelism." As he views the history of Christian expansion, relatively little has been done by professionals, except during the Protestant missionary movement of the last 175 years. The latter fitted very well the peculiar characteristics of the period — until 1960. Otherwise, Yoder says, most faith sharing has been done by migration of Christian people. And most Americans are descendents of voluntary migrants who brought their faith with them (Yoder 1961).

Of course, most migrants have moved to improve their lot: to escape oppression or to improve their economic opportunities. Yoder asks whether we couldn't now migrate for higher motivation — even though it means moving down the economic scale. This concept must have seemed rather idealistic to many of Yoder's readers in 1961, even though he was careful to augment the ideal with a good bit of realism and practical advice. But the emerging consciousness might view this concept quite positively.

In this connection, we should at least mention one other aspect of the money linkages we discussed above. In the mid-70's our economy in America has changed. This is certainly more than a cycle. It is an illness that may well spell the demise of our so-called expanding economy, hemmed in, as it now is, by both ecological and energy limit stops. Something has to give. And that something may include our privilege of sending money out of the country. Self-supporting, limited-life-style communities may, in the foreseeable future, be our only missionary option. But that need not spell the end of our here/there community links, providing we fully clarify the true basis of our relatedness. The latter is well worth working on now.

These economic trends have even more potential consequences for our presently-constituted sodalities than for our sending congregations. The same is true of the constantly-escalating cost of our present methods and life styles. But I feel there is an even more urgent reason for pushing ahead with some alternative models.

Today we are hearing a lot about Third World missions — that is, Third World churches forming mission sodalities for cross-cultural ministries. The emphasis is important and overdue. But I have one fear: that too many of these churches will mimic our models, and at a time when, according to the analysis of this book, these models are much in need of revision. While I have based much of my discussion on our changing consciousness in this country, certain elements of the new consciousness are global — particularly in urban areas. More importantly, many of the new consciousness trends are commendably radical from a truly Christian standpoint: e.g. community values vs. individualistic values; also, simpler life styles. These same examples serve to show that some of the new consciousness trends bring us closer to non-Western cultures, as Dayton Roberts pointed out (see Introduction). It would be a tragedy if by clinging to the culturally-induced deficiencies of our present models we put a stumbling block in the way of our Third World brethren. God forbid! By courageous critique of our own structures, we can provide alternative models for them to observe and apply. By example, we can help them at the same time we help ourselves.

Of course, there is yet another possibility: we may already be too late for this pace-setting role. Or, if not too late yet, we may drag our feet too long, too married to our settled way of doing things. Perhaps the Holy Spirit will guide these emerging third world mission sodalities to develop the new models, and we will have to learn from them. While I'm putting the finishing touches to this appeal to my fellow mission leaders in America, Miss Chaeok Chun, for 12 years a missionary from Korea to Pakistan, is developing her doctoral dissertation around the need of community models for Asian missions. Though our graduate studies at Fuller Seminary overlapped one academic year, her vision developed quite independently out of her own missionary experience, and, indeed, her Asian cultural perspective. Her advocacy of community-model missions may prove to be far more important than my current efforts.

Toward Enabling Structures

As I pointed out early, this is a book about structures. I also declared myself on the side of low-profile structures, and wary about the organizational trends of our society — a trend I was once deeply involved in. I hope it has been clear that I do not want to throw the baby out with the bath water. In one sense, I could not even if I wanted to. For as we've noted, structure "is". And the final question before us as we draw our study to a close is not so much the level or intensity of the structured-ness we choose, but how can we make structure serve us instead of our having to be enslaved by structural machinery.

We cannot expect any simple solutions. The trend from new "movements" to institutionalization is inexorable. "Great ventures start with a vision and end with a power structure" (Gardner 1963:131). But there are choices that can slow down (or speed up!) this process. We can only touch on these here; and we will concentrate more on attitudes than techniques.

Structures enable and facilitate vision. The structures created by vanguards of committed Christians facilitate their *shared* vision(s). These structures enable them to pursue their shared vision *together*. Normally this requires *continuing* facilitation, so structure provides that continuity. And right here is the first hazard to be negotiated. "Continuity" is relative; it may or may not have any relationship to "longevity" or "perpetuity". But the institutionalization (and American organizational) trend will move toward the latter unless conscious decision and effort is made to avoid it.

Some may wonder why this need be avoided. Isn't it a good idea to facilitate and extend a vision as long as possible? Not necessarily. Sometimes, as James Russell Lowell's hymn quaintly puts it, "Time makes ancient good uncouth." But never mind that. More often, the vision may indeed remain valid. But once we've carefully designed a *form* (in this case, a structure) to facilitate and continue that vision, we tend to "conserve" the form, which is more tangible, and therefore more manageable, than the vision. (Indeed, as time passes, we tend not even to distinguish the two.) Yet, unless the form moves with the *Zeitgeist*, it will inevitably *distort* the vision. So to actually conserve the vision, the form must change. This is a poorly-understood reality of conserve-atism, and possibly a key reason why it loses otherwise conservative adherents in a period of substantial change. I'm also concerned about the price we pay when we allow structural longevity to become a major goal. We mustn't go to the other extreme and ignore continuity. But I urge the coming new missionary communities: aim only for that degree of continuity-structure you really *need;* avoid like the plague letting "accepted" organizational practices waste your time. A truly enabling structure should free you to concentrate on vitality — to channel into current effectiveness the energy that can all too easily get dissipated in survival planning.

What we've noted about stripped-down life styles in this volume should likewise enter into structural planning. The accumulation of assets also extracts its price. Gardner maintains that this is part of the reason why "form triumphs over spirit" or vision as discussed above. "As assets expand, the ardor wanes. The buildings grow bigger and the spirit thins out" *(ibid:17)*. But most crucial of all is the relationship of assets (which include more than money) to *freedom.* "Preoccupation with conserving what we have may make us much less venturesome" and reduce our flexibility *(ibid:51ff.).*

And it's right here that we must turn from the likes of John Gardner in order to sit once again at the feet of Paul, the one who gave us the classic prototype for the small committed missionary community we're radically seeking. I sense the heart throb of this man of mobility as he cries, "I want you to be free of anxieties!" (I Cor. 7:32). Surely he doesn't limit that to the marriage/celibacy issue he was then discussing, which may have been accentuated in that context by a contemporary problem ("the impending distress," v. 26). The immediate freedom Paul "wanted" for the Corinthians was freedom from worldly entanglements. In his own life, this bred freedom to move — geographically. But probably the greatest freedom of all is the freedom to risk. This is creative freedom.

In his cultural mandate, God paid us the ultimate compliment of making us his image-bearers, including the creative impulse. But creativity demands risk. Think of the risk God took as he created us with freedom of choice — and the painful results. Yet ultimately his risk will assuredly be vindicated. And all because God so *exercised* his freedom!

In his evangelistic mandate, Jesus Christ paid us the compliment of sharing his sent-ness (John 20:21). Think of the risk he took as he voluntarily responded to his own sending (Phil. 2:7-8) — and the injustice that resulted. Yet his risk was vindicated in resurrection, and will ultimately be crowned with transcendent glory! And all because Jesus Christ exercised his freedom! Think also of the further risk he took in leaving a monumental, world-wide task to a small committed community of his followers.

Yes, my committed brothers and sisters, think about *that*. I, like Paul, want you to be *free!* Free to commit your lives unreservedly to Jesus Christ. Free to commit yourself to one another and to create valid structures for sharing your faith with all the world's unreached peoples. And then free to *go*, risking anything and everything for our Lord.

Retrospect

Looking broadly at our world today, I am tempted to get dramatic and lift a line from the late Martin Luther King. For I, too, have a dream. I've expressed at several points my expectancy — even conviction — of a coming new wave of missionary energy that will eclipse any previous one. I believe this not only because of the surfacing missionary interest I see in the young; but also because I see new evidences of receptivity among non-Christian peoples — a ripening harvest in many places.

Just as the Lord prepared Adoniram Judson and his teammates for that first overseas wave from America, and just as he prepared Hudson Taylor and his colleagues for the mid-nineteenth-century wave, and as he prepared many of us for the post-World War II wave, so I see the new consciousness being prepared. My "dream" includes not only further winning of animistic people, where we have seen most of our results to date, but also a significant penetration of the world religions. Is this the generation that will witness a break-through with Islam? I believe it is highly possible. The potential before us merits our best efforts to achieve relevant, enabling structures.

God wills the reconciliation of men to himself; he has provided for that reconciliation in Jesus Christ; and he has given us the ministry of reconciliation (II Corinthians 5:18,19). This has been a presupposition of our study. It has been a thesis of our study that this reconciling ministry has never in history been carried out by the whole People of God, but by the committed few on behalf of the many. This committed minority has been most effective in its reconciling ministry when banded together in committed communities, which have taken a wide variety of forms over the centuries. These sodalities must live in creative tension with the nurture structures of the Church, maintaining a life of their own with the freedom to exercise initiative for their evangelistic task.

It has also been a thesis of this study that our current sodality models, basically inherited from the nineteenth century, are in need of revision. All such forms are subject to subtle distortions, on the one hand, and obsolescence due to lack of up-dating, on the other. Given the significantly-changing consciousness today, structural revision or replacement of our sodality forms is particularly urgent. May God give us the vision, the wisdom and the courage to tackle this crucial task — with joy.

For Further Study

Chapter 1: Communities of the Church

Ralph Winter wrote a series of articles on structures that were later collected in a booklet called *The Warp and the Woof: Organizing for Mission* (1970). This is now out of print; a revised, re-titled edition will be published in 1977. Meanwhile, the clearest statement of his two-structure view is contained in his article, "The Two Structures of God's Redemptive Mission" (1974).

In chapter 5, I quote from the writings of Church Missionary Society leaders who have been prominent sodality apologists. The contexts of those quotes make profitable reading (Taylor 1966; Warren 1971 & 1974).

Howard Snyder (1975) takes a different, but related, approach to structure. His soon-to-be published (by Inter-Varsity Press in 1977) new book on the Church and the Kingdom probes this subject more deeply. Some of the church renewal literature brushes against this subject (e.g., Edge 1971); some of these are noted below in relation to other chapters.

Chapter 2: Committed Bands

The Bible!

Beyond the pages cited in the text, DeRidder's (1975) first two chapters provide an excellent theology of missions in the Old Testament.

Edward Murphy has dealt with the apostolic teams of the New Testament period — first in chapters 14 and 15 of his book (1975) in the context of spiritual gifts; then, more directly and briefly, in an article (1976) based on this same material.

Chapter 3: Monks and Friars

Latourette is an interesting, easy-to-read source if you don't let the size of his works scare you. Read him by subject from the index; the indexing is superb. You'll actually find him quite succinct. The 1953 volume and the 7-volume work (1970) complement each other. The first *two* volumes of the latter (the second is not listed in the Bibliography) cover this period.

Bishop Neill's paperback, *A History of Christian Missions* (1964) is a fine supplement to Latourette. Though smaller in size, it sometimes covers a given subject more adequately. The index is less comprehensive but helpful.

The late Dr. John T. McNeill spent a lifetime researching and writing about the Celtic Churches. His final book (1974) is not only up to date, but written for a wider audience; I found it positively fascinating. Steve Clark's very recent book (1976) on the earliest monastic communities is in the same category. We'll encounter another well-thought-out book by this serious-yet-readable community authority in a later chapter.

Books on Francis of Assisi are legion. By my quotes it is obvious that I found helpful a book by Joan Erikson (1970), wife of renowned psychoanalyst, Erik Erikson.

Chapter 4: Radical Christians

Littell (1958) could probably qualify as a "dean" of current Anabaptist historians. You might find him providing more than you cared to know. Durnbaugh (1968) builds much of his book (Part Two) around specific historical *models* — before, during and following the period involved. You can more easily read him selectively. Yoder's paper (1971) reviews further reading potential.

A good deal of Moravian material suffers just a bit from being authored by its own leaders. Not so with insider Bost's book (1848). It's a gem — if you can find a library that has it. Lutheran Danker (1971) helpfully focuses on the community as a mission model, while emphasizing the economic aspect of the model. The extended

Introduction in Stoeffler (1965) is a very good summary essay of how Pietism relates to our subject.

Chapter 5: Voluntary Societies

Under Chapter 1 above, I've already suggested the writings of Taylor and Warren, which include selections from Henry Venn. To this we should add the selected writings of Rufus Anderson edited by R. Pierce Beaver (1967). Though I have not cited it in the text, Beaver's 1968 treatment of the role of women in 19th century missions gives a great deal of additional insight into the whole nature of voluntarism.

Volumes 4, 5 & 6 of Latourette's *Expansion* all deal with "The Great Century." But volume 4 is the one to "browse by index" on the voluntary societies of both America and Europe.

And, by all means, read Carey's *Enquiry* in whatever edition you can find!

Chapter 6: Commitment and Consciousness

The best reflective look at the rise of the counter-culture in Christian perspective is Os Guiness' *The Dust of Death* (1973). This young intellectual combines the perspective and insights of his generation with the analytical approach of his colleague, Francis Schaeffer of L'Abri.

But don't neglect the secular analysts. Reich (1971) does not deserve to be shrugged off; admittedly his book is too long (though easy to read) and he does make you mad. Slater is the opposite: brief but difficult. One Christian magazine review referred to his second book (1974) as a kind of thinking man's Reich; a rather snobbish comment, I thought. Personally, I preferred Slater's first book (1971) and found it very helpful. But I found Roszak's first (1969) the most helpful of all.

It's really a bit late to be reading very much about the original Jesus movement, per se, but if you want a brief pulse-beat of the movement, choose Palms (1971). Williams (1972) is also brief and warm. This young-but-then-establishment Presbyterian minister got right *into* the heart of the movement, and his autobiographical account breathes authenticity. Ellwood (1973) seems a little too bent, at first, on authenticating himself to his university peers, but the latter half of the book is excellent — best reflective analysis I've read.

Most books on Christian life style are written from political perspectives that many of my readers may not share; but this does not invalidate their insights. Art Gish (1973) sticks closest to practical, personal life styles. And don't get turned off by the early chapters — he's not that simplistic throughout. Taylor (1975) spends more time on our society, but there are plenty of personal applications. And he's a superb writer.

Chapter 7: Community

If you somehow missed the relational movement, start with Larson (1971). If you want more, I'd suggest Edge (1971) next. Clark (1972) is tops on community, per se, and also on renewal through community; he sticks to his subject so objectively that I read through this book without knowing he was charismatic. As indicated in the text, the Jacksons have produced a worthy handbook on intentional Christian communities (1974).

Somewhere I must bring in Kelley (1972). Though he's dealing primarily with the diocesan structure, his chapter 8 deals with more-committed community models of the past and present. And, of course, the whole book focuses on commitment.

Chapter 8: Emerging Models

Because Operation Mobilization avoids publicity, Verwer's own book (1972) is a principal source. Happily it is not a puff or even a description but rather gives a "feel" of the movement. *To Munich with Love* (Owens 1972) probably gives the best reflection of Youth With A Mission's current self-understanding. Though I haven't read it, I suspect that the earlier little paperback, *God's Guerrillas* (Wilson 1971), may contain a less-official feel for YWAM's freer-wheeling earlier years.

McClung's book about Dilaram (1975) takes a historical approach to the young community, but still clearly conveys the heart-beat. For more information on the team approach of Phil Elkins and his colleagues see his brief article recently published (1976). He was writing on this subject more than 10 years ago, before his field service (1965:54-59); unfortunately the book is out of print.

For my purpose, it has been necessary to stick to Western (primarily American) models. But interestingly, an indigenous Anglican order, the Melanesian Brotherhood, has been a strong and effective missionary sodality of communitarian character in those islands (Tippett 1967, see his index). Biot (1963), a French Catholic, deals very ably with *The Rise of Protestant Monasticism* circa World War II in Europe, with emphasis on Taize and the Evangelical Sisterhood of Mary. Chun (1976) also deals with these European communities, the Melanesian Brotherhood, Indian Ashrams, and other emerging Asian models.

Chapter 9: Creating Committed Communities

The very title of Snyder's book, *The Problem of Wineskins* (1975) indicates his wrestlings with this problem. If you think I'm tough on the subject of the influence of money on missions, see Allen 1972:109. Allen wrote these devastating, prophetic comments in the 1920's. Yoder's little booklet is very good in thinking through the idea of migrating communities (1961).

Viewed one way, Gardner's 1963 book might seem a collection of clichés. That's his style. But from this treatise on renewing people and institutions, you can discern (by application) some practical wisdom on traps to avoid in the original structuring process. A decade ago, this book was crucial in my becoming an ex-organization man.

Bibliography

ALLEN, Roland
1972   *The Ministry of the Spirit: Selected Writings of Roland Allen,* David M. Paton, ed. Grand Rapids, Eerdmans.

BAINTON, Roland H.
1950   *Here I Stand: A Life of Martin Luther.* New York, Abingdon.

BARKER, Glenn W., LANE, William L., and MICHAELS, J. Ramsey
1969   *The New Testament Speaks.* New York, Harper & Row.

BEAVER, R. Pierce, ed.
1967   *To Advance the Gospel: Selections from the Writings of Rufus Anderson.* Grand Rapids, Eerdmans.

1968   *All Loves Excelling: American Protestant Women in World Mission.* Grand Rapids, Eerdmans.

BETTENSON, Henry, ed.
1967   *Documents of the Christian Church.* New York, Oxford University Press.

BIOT, François
1963   *The Rise of Protestant Monasticism.* Baltimore, Helicon.

BLAUW, Johannes
1962   *The Missionary Nature of the Church: A Survey of the Biblical Theology of Mission.* New York, McGraw-Hill.

BOST, A.
1848   *History of the Bohemian and Moravian Brethren.* London, The Religious Tract Society.

CABLE, Mildred, and FRENCH, Francesca
1946   *Ambassadors for Christ.* London, Paternoster Press.

CAREY, William
1961   *An Enquiry into the Obligations of Christians to Use Means for the Conversion of the Heathens,* New facsimile edition. London, The Carey Kingsgate Press Limited.

CHUN, Chaeok
1976   "An Exploration of the Community Model for Asian Missionary Outreach." An unpublished D.Miss. dissertation, School of World Mission, Fuller Theological Seminary, Pasadena.

CLARK, Stephen B.
1972   *Building Christian Communities: Strategy for Renewing the Church.* Notre Dame, Indiana, Ave Maria Press.

1976   *Unordained Elders and Renewal Communities.* New York, Paulist Press.

COOK, Harold
1971   *Historic Patterns of Church Growth: A Study of Five Churches.* Chicago, Moody Press.

COX, Harvey
1966   *The Secular City: Secularization and Urbanization in Theological Perspective.* New York, Macmillan.

DANKER, William J.
1971   *Profit for the Lord: Economic Activities in Moravian Missions and the Basel Mission Trading Company.* Grand Rapids, Eerdmans.

DE RIDDER, Richard R.
1975   *Discipling the Nations.* Grand Rapids, Baker Book House.

DOUGLAS, J.D., ed.
1975   *Let the Earth Hear His Voice, International Congress on World Evangelization, Lausanne, Switzerland.* Minneapolis, World Wide Publications

DURNBAUGH, Donald F.
1968   *The Believers' Church: The History and Character of Radical Protestantism.* New York, Macmillan.

EDGE, Finley B.
1971   *The Greening of the Church.* Waco, Texas, Word.

ELKINS, Phillip W.
1965   *Toward a More Effective Mission Work.* Dallas, Christian Publishing Co.

1974   *Church Sponsored Missionaries.* Austin, Texas, Firm Foundation Publishing House.

1976   "Church-to-Field Missionary Teams: Here's How." *Evangelical Missions Quarterly.* 12:101-106.

ELLER, Vernard
1973   *The Simple Life: The Christian Stance toward Possessions.* Grand Rapids, Eerdmans.

ELLUL, Jacques
1964   *The Technological Society*. New York, A.A. Knopf.

ELLWOOD, Robert S., Jr.
1973   *One Way: The Jesus Movement and Its Meaning*. Englewood Cliffs, N.J.,
        Prentice-Hall

ENROTH, Ronald M., ERICSON, Edward E., Jr., and PETERS, C. Breckenridge
1972   *The Jesus People: Old-Time Religion in the Age of Aquarius*. Grand Rapids,
        Eerdmans.

ERIKSON, Joan M.
1970   *Saint Francis et His Four Ladies*. New York, Norton.

GARDNER, John W.
1961   *Excellence*. New York, Harper & Row.

1963   *Self-Renewal*. New York, Harper & Row.

GISH, Arthur G.
1973   *Beyond the Rat Race*. Scottsdale, Penna., Herald Press.

GLASSER, Arthur F.
1973   "Church Growth and Theology" in *God, Man and Church Growth*, Alan R.
        Tippett, ed. Grand Rapids, Eerdmans.

GRAHAM, Billy
1971   *The Jesus Generation*. Grand Rapids, Zondervan.

GREEN, Michael
1970   *Evangelism in the Early Church*. Grand Rapids, Eerdmans.

GUINNESS, Os
1973   *The Dust of Death*. Downers Grove, Ill., Inter-Varsity Press.

HUGHES, Kathleen
1966   *The Church in Early Irish Society*. Ithaca, N.Y., Cornell University Press.

JACKSON, Dave and Neta
1974   *Living Together in a World Falling Apart: A Handbook on Christian Community*.
        Carol Stream, Illinois, Creation House.

KELLEY, Dean M.
1972   *Why Conservative Churches are Growing: A Study in Sociology of Religion*. New
        York, Harper & Row

LARSON, Bruce
1971   *No Longer Strangers*. Waco, Texas, Word.

LATOURETTE, Kenneth S.
1953   *A History of Christianity*. New York, Harper & Row.

1970a   *The First Five Centuries*. Vol. 1 of *A History of the Expansion of Christianity*.
        Grand Rapids, Zondervan.

1970b   *Three Centuries of Advance. A.D. 1500 - A.D. 1800*. Vol. 3 of *A History of the
        Expansion of Christianity*. Grand Rapids, Zondervan.

LITTELL, Franklin H.
1958   *The Anabaptist View of the Church: A Study in the Origins of Sectarian Protestantism.* Boston, Star King Press.

LUTHER, Martin
1965   *Liturgy and Hymns,* Ulrich S. Leupold, ed., Vol. 53 of *Luther's Works,* Hulmut T. Lehmann, Gen'l. ed., Philadelphia, Fortress Press.

McCLUNG, Floyd, Jr. with CONN, Charles Paul
1975   *Just Off Chicken Street.* Old Tappan, N.J., Revell.

McGAVRAN, Donald A.
1955   *The Bridges of God: A Study in the Strategy of Missions.* New York, Friendship Press.

McNEILL, John T.
1974   *The Celtic Churches: A History, A.D. 200 to 1200.* Chicago, University of Chicago Press.

McNEILL, John T. and GAMER, Helena M.
1965   *Medieval Handbooks of Penance.* New York, Octagon Books.

MURPHY, Edward F.
1975   *Spiritual Gifts and the Great Commission.* South Pasadena, Mandate Press

1976   "The Missionary Society as an Apostolic Team". *Missiology: An International Review* IV:103-118.

MURPHY, Franklin D.
1968   "The State of the University," excerpted in *The Los Angeles Times* for June 18 under headline: " 'To Do,' 'To Feel' Must be Balanced."

NEILL, Stephen
1964   *A History of Christian Missions.* Baltimore, Penguin Books.

OWENS, Bob
1972   *To Munich with Love.* Chino, Calif., Chic Publications

PALMS, Roger C.
1971   *The Jesus Kids.* Valley Forge, Pa., Judson Press.

PLOWMAN, Edward E.
1971   *The Underground Church: Accounts of Christian Revolutionaries in Action.* Elgin, Ill., David C. Cook.

REICH, Charles A.
1971   *The Greening of America.* New York, Bantam Books.

ROSZAK, Theodore
1969   *The Making of a Counter Culture: Reflections on the Technocratic Society and its Youthful Opposition.* New York, Doubleday (Anchor Books).

1973   *Where the Wasteland Ends: Politics and Transcendence in Post-Industrial Society.* Garden City, N.Y., Doubleday (Anchor Books).

SLATER, Philip
1971   *The Pursuit of Loneliness: American Culture at the Breaking Point.* Boston, Beacon Press.

1974   *Earthwalk.* New York, Anchor Press/Doubleday.

SNYDER, Howard A.
1975   *The Problem of Wine Skins: Church Structure in a Technological Age.* Downers Grove, Illinois, Inter-Varsity Press.

SPARKS, Jack
1974   *God's Forever Family.* Grand Rapids, Zondervan.

STEDMAN, Ray C.
1972   *Body Life.* Glendale, Calif., Regal Books.

STOEFFLER, F. Ernest
1965   *The Rise of Evangelical Pietism:* Vol. IX in *Studies in the History of Religions.* Leiden, E.J. Brill.

TAYLOR, John V.
1966   *For All the World: The Christian Mission in the Modern Age.* Philadelphia, Westminster.

1975   *Enough is Enough.* London, SCM Press.

TIME Magazine
1971   "The Jesus Revolution". June 21, 1971, 56-63.

TIPPETT, Alan R.
1967   *Solomon Islands Christianity.* South Pasadena, William Carey Library.

TOWNSEND, Robert
1970   *Up the Organization: How to Stop the Corporation from Stifling People and Strangling Profits.* New York, Alfred A. Knopf.

TRUEBLOOD, Elton
1961   *The Company of the Committed.* New York, Harper & Row.

VERWER, George
1972   *Come! Live! Die! The Real Revolution.* Wheaton, Tyndale House.

WARREN, Max, ed.
1971   *To Apply the Gospel: Selections from the Writings of Henry Venn.* Grand Rapids, Eerdmans.

WARREN, Max
1974   *Crowded Canvas: Some Experiences of a Lifetime.* London, Hodder & Stoughton.

WEBSTER's Dictionary
1941   *Webster's Collegiate Dictionary,* Fifth Edition. Springfield, Mass., G. & C Merriam Co.

1966   *Webster's New World Dictionary of the American Language,* College Edition. New York, World.

WILLIAMS, Don
1972   *Call to the Streets,* Minneapolis, Augsburg.

1975   Interview with author. February 17, 1975.

WILLIAMS, George H.
1962   *The Radical Reformation.* Philadelphia, Westminster.

WILSON, R. Marshall
1971   *God's Guerrillas.* Plainfield, N.J., Logos International.

WINTER, Ralph D. and BEAVER, R. Pierce
1970   *The Warp and the Woof: Organizing for Mission.* South Pasadena, Calif., William Carey Library.

WINTER, Ralph D.
1974   "The Two Structures of God's Redemptive Mission," *Missiology: An International Review.* (January) 121-139.

YODER, John Howard
1961   *As You Go: the Old Mission in a New Day.* Scottdale, Pennsylvania, Herald Press.

1971   "Reformation and Missions: A Literature Review." *Occasional Bulletin,* Vol. XXII, No. 6, New York, Missionary Research Library.

Index

About the Author

Charles Mellis grew up in a very mission-minded church. Both his father and mother developed a strong interest in overseas activities; their home was always open to visiting missionaries, giving him and his three older sisters a personalized, in-depth exposure to Christian witness overseas. This exposure was considerably broadened in 1937 when he accompanied his father on a six-month trip through Africa, driving from Lagos to Mombassa and from Beira to Cape Town, visiting 75 mission locations. After high school he joined his father in the family business for two years, attended Wheaton College, and served as a pilot in the Army Air Force during WW II.

In 1945 he married Claire Schoolland of Boulder, Colorado; a few months later he and his bride joined with other Christian airmen who had recently formed the Mission Aviation Fellowship. He served 27 years as an executive officer of this mission service agency, his last three years as president. While most of this service was at the Southern California headquarters, in 1952 the family, including three sons, John, James and Gordon, embarked on a three-year term in New Guinea, developing several air services in both political subdivisions of that large island. A fourth son, Gilbert, was born there. Later in the 1950's the family spent another year abroad involving survey and development work in Central Africa and several Pacific islands. The birth of Esther in 1963 completed the Mellis family.

During the five-year period, 1968-1973, he participated in a planned transition of MAF's leadership into the hands of a younger management team. Following this, he pursued his MA in Missiology at the School of World Mission, Fuller Theological Seminary, Pasadena.

Currently he serves as Director of the Summer Institute of International Studies, as Assistant Editor of *Missiology, An International Review,* and as an adjunct professor of missions. He also serves on the boards of three mission agencies and as a consultant to several mission-related groups.